Hometown Memories

The Journal

Hometown Memories

Growing Up in Martinsburg, West Virginia

Collected Writings

of

Ethel Wayble Bovey

Mountain State Publishing Services
Martinsburg, West Virginia

Hometown Memories

Growing Up in Martinsburg, West Virginia

Grateful acknowledgment is made to The Journal Publishing Company for permission to use works of the author that first appeared in *The Journal*, the daily newspaper of Martinsburg, West Virginia.

ISBN 0-9747005-0-9

Published in the United States by
Mountain State Publishing Services
70 Whitings Neck Road
Martinsburg, West Virginia 25401

II

Cover

Martinsburg's Public Square in the early 1900s.
Back cover, left to right: the Berkeley Hotel, County Court House, view of Queen Street facing north.
Front cover, left to right: the Continental Hotel, the Band Stand, the Women's Club.

Frontispiece

Ethel Bovey relaxing at home in Martinsburg in 2003 with a copy of *The Journal*, the hometown newspaper for which she has written since 1963. The photo was taken by the Boys Club of Martinsburg.

This book is dedicated to
my husband Max
and our daughter Sharilyn
for their unfailing love
and encouragement
through the years.

Acknowledgments

I must mention my mentor, the late Paul Buxton (Buck) Martin, editor of *The Martinsburg Journal,* who first gave me the opportunity to write for publication. Grateful appreciation also goes to my special friends Kathy Weaver and Maxine Newbraugh, who have insisted, even nagged me to publish my writings; and last but certainly far from least, my friend and former coworker at *The Journal,* Peggy May McClurken, now the publisher who is making my dream a reality.

I extend a special note of thanks to Craig Bohrer and The Journal Publishing Company for generously granting permission to reprint these stories, most of which first appeared in slightly different form in *The Journal.*

I am especially grateful to Don Wood and the Berkeley County Historical Society for graciously lending many of the wonderful old photographs that supplement and complement the text in this book.

I would also like to mention Jane Levitan, public relations coordinator of the Martinsburg-Berkeley County Public Library. Unable to locate a suitable updated library photo to include, she went right out and took one and sent it to my publisher the same day! Likewise, Bob and Ruth Ann Dean responded on short notice and supplied a wonderful photograph of Bob's grandfather, John W. Dean, to add life to a story written almost four decades ago.

Finally, I thank my family and friends for their unending support, and I extend admiration and appreciation to all those people whose stories and deeds throughout the years made this book possible.

My goal is to leave something to tell future generations about the life we lived while we were here. This book is not intended to be a history, but a collection of informal chats about life and some of the people in Martinsburg during my lifetime. Readers who have shared those years may enjoy re-living some of them, and those who come along later may learn a few things about us they would like to know.

Contents

Editor's Note

Time and again in the course of this book's road to publication, as I read these stories of everyday people, I was reminded of the greatness of simplicity. For these are stories of men and women who suffered great losses yet treasured small pleasures, of laborers who worked hard but always had time for their neighbors, of entrepreneurs and concerned citizens who had visions of a better Martinsburg and refused to allow obstacles to stand in their way. Their lives are made even more special by a storyteller who laughed and cried, labored and loved, lived and dreamed right along with them.

Through the years, Ethel Bovey has told many stories, charming her audiences with her humor, amazing all with her acuity. Her writing reflects the underlying pride she feels for her hometown. It radiates her genuine concern for people. It captures her unwavering love of God, of writing, and of life.

To say Ethel is a local legend would not be an overstatement. In the course of her career, she has been an inspiration to many, this writer included. Undaunted by the competitive nature of journalism, she stands out in her profession as a friend and helper to all aspiring writers and editors.

I first met Ethel more than 30 years ago when I was a fledgling new hire to *The Journal* news staff with the dubious task of succeeding her as women's editor while she moved up to the position of feature editor. She took me under her protective wing and patiently nurtured me in the fine art of reporting the activities of Martinsburg society and the ins and outs, dos and don'ts of small town "newspapering." I wasn't a unique case; she did the same for countless others who came along later. Here are a few tributes to her greatness, sentiments I echo wholeheartedly:

> **I have known Ethel Bovey for my entire 23-year career as a journalist and public relations practitioner. Ethel served as a mentor to me when I was new to the business and has remained a strong supporter of this newspaper and me personally for more than 20 years. I can't say enough about her commitment to the profession. She remains knowledgeable and enthusiastic about her career to this day. She still writes a column for us on a regular basis, when she's not traveling.**
>
> **Ethel is one of those people to whom you can turn with any question about local news, local people, local events, local history. She is a wonderful source. Additionally, she is a strong, faith-filled Christian woman whom I greatly admire. Over the years, she balanced her work with being a wife and a mother, something I continue to struggle with daily.**
>
> **My professional and personal life has been blessed because of Ethel. I greatly appreciate her.**
>
> **—MARIA LORENSEN, Editor, *The Journal***

> **Whenever I count the blessings I have enjoyed in my career, the first on my list is Ethel Bovey.**
>
> **She taught me not only the basics of interviewing, writing and editing but also the importance of integrity, fairness and accuracy. From Ethel I learned that journalists have a responsibility to tell a story truthfully and without opinion.**
>
> **Ethel also taught me the joy of telling a story. Throughout the years, she has told many. Her gift with words, her ability to recognize that everyone has a story to tell and her willingness to tell it, has entertained and informed countless readers.**
>
> **—LIZ THOMPSON, City Editor, *The Morning Herald***

When Ethel came to work for *The Journal* many years ago, I saw right away she was a natural for the position. She really likes people and remembers facts about places and events. Ethel always has a positive outlook on life and has never been one to complain. She has always been more interested in the welfare of others than herself. I think a lot of her.

—BILL THOMPSON, former Managing Editor, *The Journal*

Ethel and I go back many years, and she is truly an accomplished writer, well-known and articulate. She focuses on history and current events, culture and religion. Bookshelves will undoubtedly be enriched with the publication of *Hometown Memories,* where she brings together her many years of writing into a publication to be shared by everyone.

—MAXINE NEWBRAUGH, former correspondent, *The Journal*

Still another testament to the high regard the community holds for Ethel was the outpouring of support and cooperation we received for this book project. *The Journal,* without hesitation, granted us permission to reprint Ethel's stories in *Hometown Memories.* The Berkeley County Historical Society opened their files and allowed us to reproduce many wonderful old photographs, which appear throughout the pages of this book. The Public Library, City Hospital, *The Journal,* and the family of John W. Dean all responded to requests for information and pictures, sometimes on short notice. And everywhere, the response was the same: "Oh, I know Ethel. I remember the time she. . . ." Then they would tell about a funny motivational talk Ethel had given or a community function she had attended, notepad and camera in hand. For all this support, we are eternally grateful.

Ralph Waldo Emerson once wrote: "Every great and commanding movement in the annals of the world is a triumph of enthusiasm." I have to wonder if the Emerson of yesteryear had a direct line to a future Martinsburg when he wrote those words back in the nineteenth century, so close do they come to describing Ethel's *Hometown Memories*. Through her writing, Ethel challenges each of us to step back and contemplate the wonders around us during this brief span of time we are here. Through her example, she inspires us to be thankful for all that we are and excited about all that we do. Ethel's positive outlook radiates outward and seems to touch everyone she comes into contact with.

Ethel Bovey is a triumph of enthusiasm, and I will always be grateful for that fateful day my path crossed hers and allowed me to become a part of her *Hometown Memories*.

—Peggy May McClurken

Hometown Memories

Introduction

Memory is not a single golden filament, but is made up of separate links of varying degrees of importance. These links are not always easy to find. Each must be carefully searched out, polished with remembrance until the luster gleams, then given its rightful place in the chain.

The stories of my life are related in a series of recollections touching upon the town where I was born and grew up and the people who played a part in my life and in the community. These stories—revised for this book—first appeared in a column and a series of features that I wrote while working for *The Martinsburg Journal* and after my retirement.

I was born at the family home on Frederick Street in Martinsburg, third child of Wilbur and Anna Weber Wayble. Their first two daughters, Frances and Nellie May, died in childhood, thus I grew up as an only child.

Frederick Street was my world. It was just one block long, reaching from Oscar See's field at the East to Hooge Street School at the West. Papa grew up on Frederick Street too, just two doors from our home, and he and his sisters and brothers and my sister Frances all attended Hooge Street School, although it had undergone some renovation and additions.

Streets have personalities, and ours was no exception. It was a blend of the people who lived there. Each family made its own contribution. Oscar See, who lived across the street, was our horticulture expert. He grew huge, gorgeous dahlias, and people came from miles around to admire them, and to purchase them.

Mrs. See, called "Miss Fannie" by us youngsters, admired the flowers but lacked her husband's know-how. She used to tell of having once cooked a handful of tulip bulbs with a skillet of fried potatoes, and she laughed until she wiped the tears from her eyes as she told it. She didn't do a lot of cooking because her mother, Mrs. Shores, lived with them and took care of the meal preparation. It's probably best that she did!

I couldn't wait to start school, and felt really grownup the day I was taken to Dr. Eagle's office for my smallpox vaccination. Ruth Mills, a fourth-grader, took me to school the first day. Mama didn't want to take me because she had taken Frances and Frances cried so hard when she left her that she didn't want to go through that again. But I was really excited to be there.

Miss Ethel Hollida was my first grade teacher, and I thought she was the smartest lady I'd ever seen. She wore such pretty

Photo courtesy Berkeley County Historical Society

Fifth Ward School, commonly known as Hooge Street School, where Ethel attended classes as a youngster.

dresses and always had a colorful pin at the neck of her dress. When she called the roll every morning I'd answer proudly, "pres'dent," and I told Mama that Della Hill in the next row would always say, "present." I thought that was funny. But Mama asked, "And what do you say?" I responded that I said, "pres'dent, of course!" Well, the family thought it was hilarious that I thought I was president of the first grade! I think I decided that year that I wanted to be a teacher.

When I was eleven years old, the Hines family bought the vacant lot across the street from us and built a home. The parents, Jim and Virgie, had two daughters, Ruth, nine, and Ethelmae, seven, and a son, Fred, five. By this time the Mills sisters, who had been my early playmates, had moved away, and I was really glad to have the Hines girls. Of course, we just tolerated Fred. He was a nice enough little boy, but after all, a BOY, and boys didn't fit into our scheme of things.

That reminds me of the Wa-Be-Hi Club. The first chapter of the Wa-Be-Hi Club was formed on Frederick Street. It started small. We had four members: Laura Belle Bender, Ruth and Ethelmae Hines and, of course, me. The club was named by combining the first two letters of each of our family names. We made our own badges, embroidered in bright colors and worn with pride. Our club didn't grow fast. In fact, it didn't grow slowly—or at all for that matter—but it was consistent. We started with four members and we kept them. It gave us an excuse for getting together. I might add that when I retired from *The Journal* many years later, a flower arrangement arrived signed "Best Wishes from the Wa-Be-Hi Club." Needless to say, my composure was shattered.

The houses on our street were not fancy or large, but each was a comfortable home with its own neat plot of grass and flower beds and a vegetable garden in the back.

We had a porch swing, where on a summer day the neighbors could sit out and talk and get a breath of cool air. I saved up funny incidents of the school day to share when I got home, and told these things out on the porch where perhaps Miss Fannie or one of the other neighbors would be visiting.

If my mother had finished the dress she was making, I tried it on, looked at myself in the mirror and stood impatiently while she bit off a few last threads. Then, walking on air, I headed out to show it to the neighbors.

From house to house I went, for on that street we shared all our pleasures with one another. Not one mother was too busy to stop and look at it, examining it closely and admiring the work in it, for my mother was known to be a good seamstress. In fact, I was dressed from the skin out in things she had made, from the lace-trimmed bleached muslin or fine lawn underwear to the new dress I modeled with such pride.

By the time I got back home, she was rolling out dough on the kitchen table and cutting out flat dumplings to add to the pot boiling on the cookstove. I begged a couple of the dumplings, wiped a spot on a stove lid and laid them on it, then stood and watched them brown. When they were ready, I lifted them off with a knife and cautiously (for they were hot!) nibbled them.

I went upstairs, took off the new dress, and hung it smoothly on a hanger for tomorrow, putting on an everyday dress. Dresses were in three categories—Sunday dresses, school dresses and everyday dresses—and there was no mixing them up.

By that time my dad was home and we settled down to a supper of potatoes and dumplings (his favorite) cooked with ham and served with homemade apple butter and biscuits, garden lettuce with homemade dressing, sliced tomatoes, coffee and iced tea. Not a fancy menu, but how good!

After supper I took off with my books to study with Ruth and Ethelmae. There was always time left for fun after the lessons. We went out and played prisoner's base under the street light or sat on the front steps and talked. More plans were made, more simple, uncomplicated conversations enjoyed in this setting than can be imagined.

When the porchlight across the street flashed, I knew it was bedtime, and I went home and got ready. Raleigh Stewart, another neighbor and my father's special friend, was more than likely there, and the two of them sat laughing and talking together in the swing. There always seemed to be a lot of laughter when those two got together.

I said my prayers and settled down in bed for the night. The last sounds I heard were the men's voices drifting into the window over the porch. It was a comforting sound.

Somehow, there entered my childish mind the realization that here was security. Here on this street, my small world, was all that was needed for a good life. Here I was accepted for myself. I was loved and wrapped in the warmth of friendship. Life was good. I turned over and went to sleep.

Photo from author's collection

A later-years photo of Ethel's early family home on Frederick Street in Martinsburg. She remembers a one-block-long street where each family contributed to the "personality" of the close-knit neighborhood.

Long-Ago Times

Christmas Memories

Adapted from ***The Journal***
January 19, 2000

A beautifully decorated tree and dolls always come to mind when I think of Christmas, so I'll share some memories of both. Little girls today have many more interests than playing with dolls, but in my childhood her doll was the center of a little girl's play activity.

Today's child gets up on Christmas morning and finds under the tree the doll she's been longing for ever since she first saw it walking across the television screen or doing any of the myriad other things it does. She knows in advance that it's a Tillie Toddler, a Betty Burps, a Pouting Polly or a Debbie Dribbler. She's already acquainted with the doll and well informed of its talents.

It's so fully mechanized that when a cord is pulled or a button pressed it will respond perfectly. Chances are it has an electronic device inside that will speak sentences in sequence or at random. Tears will flow down its cheeks—it will drink—it will wet—it will walk stiff-legged about the room. In a few days or weeks it will have proved itself and performed these few accomplishments over and over and over. Small wonder that in a short while the little mother will have completely lost interest in her doll.

We were much more fortunate when I was a child. There were a number of dolls in my life. Gertrude, Anna Louise (named for my mother), Helen, Bonnie Jean, and Barbara Jane are a few that come to mind.

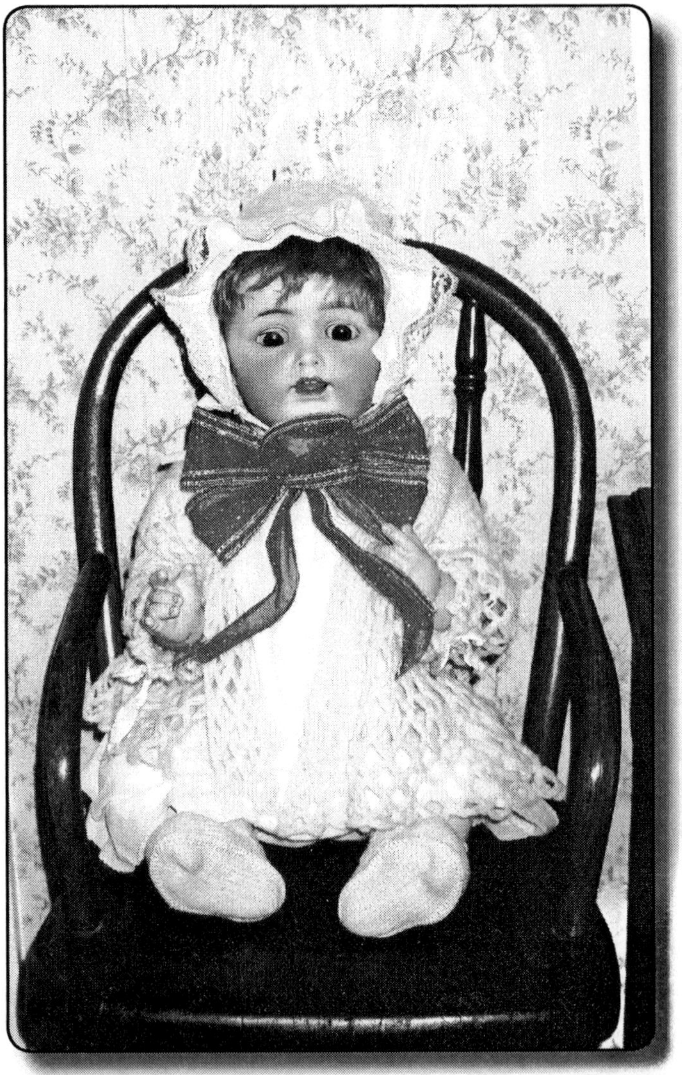

Photo from author's collection

Ethel's "Bonnie Jean." A childhood Christmas present, Bonnie Jean still has a place in Ethel's heart and home today. Ethel remembers her dolls as prized possessions when she was growing up.

Bonnie Jean was shipped from Los Angeles as a gift from a cousin who moved there when I was small. She was beautiful and much admired by all, but spent much of her time in the box as a prized possession, so I still have her.

But I think I'll tell you about Barbara Jane, for she was the last one received and holds a special place in my heart. I first met her when she smiled at me from the window of Harry Wilson's grocery store on Hooge Street. Ordinarily, Mr. Wilson didn't carry dolls, and I don't know why he did that year. But there she was in her pink dress and bonnet, her blonde hair in bangs and a fairly long cut. She stood 29 inches tall, and was plump and soft, as a doll should be. On one side of her was a similar, dark-haired doll in blue, and on the other a brunette dressed in pink. But I had eyes only for her.

I went home star-struck and told my parents about her, hoping that she could be mine, but met with no encouragement. After all, I was 11 years old, almost too old for dolls. A few days later, she disappeared from the window, and I was heartsick. I decided I'd settle for one of the others, but she would never be as dear.

As you might have guessed, on Christmas morning there she was—a gift from my parents—and my happiness knew no bounds. I can still remember the thrill of seeing my mother carrying her down the stairs. She was every bit as cuddly as I knew she would be. I held her dimpled hands, gave her a slight, almost imperceptible lift from one side at a time, and she walked in baby gait before me across the floor. I named her Barbara Jane and called her Bobbie Jane.

She had no mechanical insides, no whiny or rasping voice repeating phrases. She had no batteries and needed none. She had only a small cylinder somewhere within that enabled her to say "Mama" in a pleasing voice, but I didn't really even need that. We didn't depend upon gadgetry to make our dolls real. We almost breathed life into them.

In a short time after receiving them, they were our inseparable companions. So it was with Bobbie Jane. She wore clothing my mother made—a woolen coat with matching beret, white mittens fashioned from the tops of a pair of socks, and her own real baby shoes and socks.

When she wasn't walked or being carried about the house, she sat in her reed stroller or my little rocking chair. Perhaps because I grew up as an only child she was dearer to me than she would have been otherwise. But she was there to share my happy moments or smile with sympathy or encouragement when needed.

She went with me across the street to play with Ruth Hines and her Betty Antoinette. When we went anywhere as a family, she went right along, dressed for the weather, and on particularly cold days, with a blanket tucked about her in the stroller.

Bobbie Jane was unique only to me, because she was mine. It was this way with the dolls of my friends. Dolls took on the personalities of their small mothers. I remember Laura Belle Bender's Emma Jane. She was dressed in full, ruffled petticoats, had long dark curls about her shoulders, and sat primly in Laura Belle's mother's tiny rocker.

So it was with dolls those days. We were very fortunate. We achieved a rapport with them that was not dependent upon the whims of a manufacturer. Their talents were not limited to mechanics or batteries—and they lasted as long as we needed them. Many years later I gave Bobbie Jane to a little girl who needed a doll, but she still has a special place in my memory.

Two facts came to mind while I was thinking about this story. First of all, I mentioned that dolls were very important to little girls then, but this does not seem as true today. We grew up seeing women as mothers and homemakers, so naturally we saw nurturing and homemaking as our future. Few professional fields were open to women. Those were the years of the Great Depression, and many women saw their future as finding a job until they met the "man of their dreams" as portrayed in films of the era, then marrying and raising a family. We were the last of the romantic generations. For the most part, we still believed there was a man out there somewhere who was meant just for us, and that sooner or later we'd meet him. He would be the love of our life, we'd marry him and have his children.

Motherhood was the ideal. This is a fact not usually understood by today's young women, who have the doors of opportunity open to them and start early to plan a career. Often, motherhood and nurturing are far from their thoughts. Additionally, today's girls participate more in sports and games that weren't considered proper then, so dolls and playing house have taken a back seat.

The second thing that came to mind was that in those days Santa was asked for only one gift. Deciding what that would be required a lot of thought. There was always one special request, followed by "and candy and nuts and oranges." It's mind-boggling today to hear the answer to the question, "What do you want Santa Claus to bring you?" In our more affluent society, he receives a long list of things. I wonder if these are appreciated as much as the one, much-longed-for gift he brought us.

Another cherished memory of my childhood is the Christmas tree. A beautifully decorated tree, with its brightly colored balls, tinsel and glowing lights has been the symbol of Christmas for centuries. Selecting and putting up just the right tree can be quite an adventure.

I'll tell you about some of the trees I remember. The first was when I was very young. My parents told me I was about four years old, but I remember it quite vividly. We always bought a fat cedar tree from someone who came by with a load of them, and to me they were beautiful. My parents trimmed our tree and arranged a yard underneath.

But what I remember most about the tree that year was watching them strip off its trimmings and take it out the door. Next thing I knew, I looked out the window and saw it lying in the yard engulfed in flames! Well, the tears flowed freely as I cried, "Poor Tiss'n tree! Poor Tiss'n tree!" I don't remember the pronunciation, (that's the way they told me I said it) but I well recall the sight. They never let me witness that sad scene again.

We had some unusual experiences with trees after Max and I were married. There was the year my sister-in-law Pauline came up from Fairfax and said pink trees were in vogue in her area. People were spraying their live trees pink and decorating them in gold, silver or pastels, and everyone thought they were breathtakingly lovely.

Well, I wasn't to be outdone—we'd have a pink tree too. So I brought up a can of paint I found in the basement and got Max to spray our tree. Strictly speaking, it wasn't really pink. It was more of a coral shade. By the time the tree was painted, it appeared more of a rust color. In fact, it looked as though it had died in the forest. Rather than smelling like the spruce it was, it smelled like paint. I decided I could remedy that, so I sprayed it with pine spray. As a result, we had a tree that looked dead, and smelled like a freshly cleaned bathroom.

Another year, we decided to put our tree in a corner of the living room instead of in front of the dining room windows at the front of the house. It looked beautiful, but from outside you couldn't even tell we had a tree. So one day while Max was at work and Sharilyn at school, I cleared the decorations from underneath and moved the tree, trimmings and all, the length of the living room to the dining room and put it in front of the windows, where it could spread Christmas cheer to passersby. When Max and Sharilyn came home they were really surprised. Max said, "Well! It's hard to tell where we'll find it when we come home tomorrow!"

One year while Sharilyn was in Shepherd College, she helped to put up and decorate the tree for the Music Department in McMurran Hall. It was quite large, of course, and she was very enthusiastic about the experience. Shortly after, she and I went out to look for a tree for our house, and I'm afraid she had the Shepherd College tree too vividly in mind. We'd always been accused of bringing home the forest, but that year we did find a dandy big tree and we brought it home with pride. Max was less than enthusiastic when he saw our choice, since he would be the one most in charge of putting it up.

He put it in the heavy iron stand he'd had made several years before and started to stand it up in front of the windows in the living room. We helped and finally got it standing. Max was tightening the bolts to hold it in place, when suddenly it toppled over with him underneath. Sharilyn and I took one look at the huge tree lying out into the room with a pair of work shoes sticking out from under—and that did it! We both just doubled up in silent laughter, hands over our faces. I don't know how he knew, but I can still hear him saying calmly, "All right! Stop laughing and pick it up!"

We did, and he got up and stepped back while she and I held onto the tree. "Is it straight?" we asked. "Yes," he replied, "Now just stand there and hold it for two weeks." I always said if our marriage survived putting up the Christmas tree I knew it would last another year. But the funny thing is, every year after the work was done, the boxes had been carried back to the basement, and the lights were glowing, we all agreed it was the prettiest tree we'd ever had.

There were other episodes of toppling trees. One fell over after we'd gone to bed the night we decorated it. Another crashed down when we had just finished trimming it and I reached behind it to turn off the lights.

Another year, I decided to spray some "flocking" on the tree to achieve a snow effect. Just as I started to work, the furnace blower came on—and I had flocking all over the dining room. Never tried that again.

I think I made local history the year I exchanged a Christmas tree. We'd bought it from E. C. Alther's on Winchester Avenue, but when I got it home it looked too small. I went back and asked if they exchanged trees. They said they never had but didn't know why not—so I got a bigger tree.

I had one mishap involved with taking down the tree. We untrimmed it and Max took it out the front door, leaving me with broom and dustpan, sweeping the needles onto a newspaper to carry to the waste can in the kitchen. I completely forgot the large braided rug rolled up across the living room floor. Sharilyn was coming downstairs and saw what she calls a scene frozen in time: her mother walking, arms outstretched with a newspaper full of pine needles and headed for the rolled-up rug. There wasn't a moment to warn me. I tripped over the rug and needles and I headed for the floor. When Max came back in, I was busily sweeping up needles at the opposite end of the room and Sharilyn was almost hysterical with laughter.

Our last live tree was bought the year of our holiday cruise. Max and I went to a tree farm and selected it, had it cut, brought it home and put it in water. We watered it faithfully after it was up, but I don't think it drank a cupful. We had bare floors at that time, and when we walked through the room we could hear the needles dropping. By the time Christmas came, we knew it had to come down. We were to leave the day after Christmas, so we took it down. By the time we got it outside it was almost bare.

That did it. We bought an artificial tree, and have used one ever since, buying a new and improved one every few years. They're lovely and can save a lot of wear and tear on the nervous system and maybe your marriage. And every year after the work is done, we exclaim, "It's the prettiest tree we've ever had!"

Those Magic Moments

Recalling Saturday nights downtown

Adapted from ***The Journal***

Downtown Martinsburg. Those two words might leave you cold when I mention them today. But I want to tell you what a magical place it was when I was growing up. It will probably sound like fantasy to you but, I assure you, it's true—every word.

We waited all week for Saturday night because that was when the stores stayed open until 10 P.M. and most of the family's shopping was done. This was necessary partly because people worked a 10-hour day, many of them six days a week, and the stores were closed on Sunday. There was no other time the family could go out together to shop.

The streets were lighted by the "white way" lamps, five large round white globes on each tall green standard, made by Matthews Foundry—gone now, of course.

But the stores! You wouldn't believe! Katz's Department Store, Emmert's Store for Women, M. Cohen & Son, The Hub, Houseworth & Zimmerman, Thompson & Thompson for men, Garner's Lady's Shop, The Union Store, Mantz's Tobacco Box with the wooden cigar Indian out front, The Lace Store, Kirson's, Eyerly's, Louis Lipsic's, J. C. Penney, Johnson's Shoe Store, Tavenner's Book Store, Roy Harrison's, Ripple's Book Store.

Not one, not two, but three five-and-ten-cent stores, Newberry's, Woolworth's, and McCrory's. There were at least two automotive supply stores, the Julias, Chriss's, Snow White and City restaurants, Criswell Florist, Silco, Peoples Drug Store, Patterson's Drug Store, L. A. Roberts Jewelry Store—the latter two still operating. This is only a partial list; if you were around here then, you undoubtedly can add more.

Movies! We had the Strand at the present location of City Hall, The Apollo on Martin Street, the Central on Burke Street and the State on King Street. You bought a striped paper bag of popcorn at George Ashton's stand at the corner of Queen and Martin or Burke streets and took off to get huge entertainment for your money at any of the four theaters.

You saw a main feature, a comedy (not a cartoon but a real slapstick with Harold Lloyd, Buster Keaton, Laurel and Hardy or some of the other really funny guys), a newsreel and a serial, all for your 15 or 25 cents admission.

The first block of West Burke Street right off Queen was filled with wagons and trucks backed up to the curb. Here the farmers brought their products for a fantastic market. You could buy just about anything you can think of: homemade bread, rolls, cakes and pies, apple butter, jellies and pickles, potato salad, cole slaw, chickens, fresh fruits, vegetables and, yes, meats. And inside the market house were supplies of the more tropical fruits not available locally.

And people! There were crowds from the afternoon until the stores began to close. Boys and girls got acquainted, walking up and down the two main blocks of downtown. Introductions were pretty casual, for growing up in the same town almost made you acquainted. You knew nearly everybody. If they weren't your schoolmates, chances were you knew someone in their family or a friend of yours did. Women shopped while men stood in doorways and talked. There was a certain small-town charm, small-town security—a precious commodity seldom found on the street today.

However, I believe some of that small town feeling can be regained. It won't be easy, and it won't happen in a week or two—but I believe it can happen. We have citizens with vision—if we'll only hear their plans and work with them for the betterment of our community. We need to shed the feeling that big is always bet-

Photo courtesy Berkeley County Historical Society

Saturday nights in downtown Martinsburg were once an exciting time, Ethel recalls, with an impressive assortment of stores and theaters and a weekly outpouring of people.

Photo courtesy Berkeley County Historical Society

The Old Market House, corner of Burke and Queen streets, was a busy place where farmers brought their produce. The market operated until 1921, when the structure was remodeled for use as store rooms and city offices.

ter, and that we must destroy the old—just tear it down and build something new and forget it—move everything out of town and let the downtown rot away. That's not positive thinking, not real progress. But that attitude can win out if we are not careful—and we'll be the losers.

Progress can be a blessing, but we need to take a look at our gains and losses. Sometimes it seems that for every gain we lose something we can never retrieve. So let's try not to let downtown Martinsburg live only in memory.

The Big "Boom"

The story behind Martinsburg's noisy nickname

Adapted from ***The Journal***
January 6, 1981

I've been asked several times recently why a particular area of Martinsburg is referred to as the "Boom." When this question came my way some years ago, I sought information from two local sources and found it to be an interesting story.

For many years, *The Journal* ran a column called *"Martinsburg in the Past"* and later *"Eastern Panhandle in the Past."* It listed happenings under such sub-heads as "Forty Years Ago," "Thirty Years Ago," etc., going back to *The Journal's* founding in May 1907. This revived memories in some readers and prompted queries from others, leading to interesting stories going back into local history.

We owe our first information about the name of the "Boom" to a listing under "Seventy Years Ago," in the *"Panhandle in the Past"* column of January 6, 1981. It read, "Electric lights are turned on for the first time in the Southwest section of Martinsburg known as the 'Boom.'" This would make the date of that important event January 6, 1911.

I found two valuable sources of information—Paul Buxton (Buck) Martin, former editor of *The Journal*, and Fern Osborne Grove, longtime resident of Winchester Avenue. Unfortunately, both are since deceased.

Buck's information was provided from his lifelong interest in local history and Fern's from personal experience. I learned that development of the "Boom" section of Martinsburg began in the 1890s when a group of forward-thinking local men interested in manufacturing and industrial development in Martinsburg organized a loan and improvement business, the Martinsburg Mining, Manufacturing and Improvement Company (MMM&I).

George Meade Bowers, an orchardist and businessman who later became a congressman from this district, was president. Others were Newton D. Baker, a local physician whose son became Secretary of War; H. C. Berry, a merchant and businessman; George W. Buxton, Martin's maternal grandfather who established a steam brick plant here in 1895; Frank E. Wilson, and Charles James Faulkner. Faulkner later became a United States Senator.

Martinsburg's population at that time numbered about 8,000, and the principal industries were the Kilbourn Knitting Machine Company, later the Interwoven Stocking Company, and still later known as Martinsburg Mills, employing some 1,100 people and recognized as the largest men's hosiery factory in the world; the Crawford Woolen Mill, later employing 500 as the Berkeley Woolen Company; Brooklyn Brass Manufacturing Company, in a portion of what was later Martinsburg Mills; the Auburn Wagon Works on West Race Street, which produced wagons, shipped them to all parts of the world, and according to records of the time, employed "scores of skilled mechanics;" and the Berkeley Pants Company, with more than 100 employees.

Hannisville Distillery, located in the plant which later housed the National Fruit Product Company on North Queen Street, was in full operation, as was the Canning and Cold Storage Company in the Cassco Ice Company (now Reddy Ice) location on Rothwell Avenue. This plant was begun locally by Jim Rothwell about 1875 because of the need for cold storage for apples. Also, Standard Lime & Stone Company operated two extensive kilns and H. McDowell, one kiln.

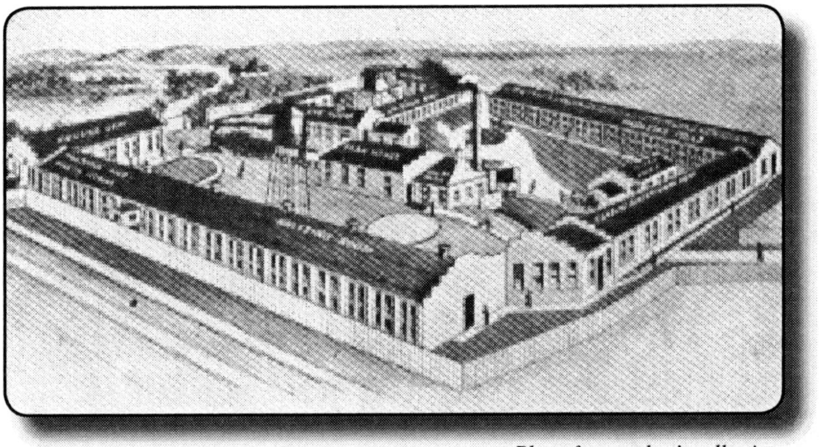

Photo from author's collection

The rapid development of manufacturing and industrial factories, such as the Martinsburg Mills shown here, resulted in what has been referred to as the "Boom" section of Martinsburg.

There were many businesses and wholesale and retail establishments, and with this growth, housing became a vital need. Thus the MMM&I was formed.

The area selected for residential housing development was bounded by South Raleigh Street on the east and Winchester Avenue on the west and extended south to Wilson Street or Elkins Park.

I'll bet that perked up your ears. Never heard of Elkins Park? Well, neither had I. The streetcar line (yes, that's right, streetcar line) ran out South Raleigh to Elkins Park, a favorite recreational and picnic spot for families to take packed lunches, go to the park on the streetcar and spend the day. The park was named for United States Senator Stephen B. Elkins, a resident of Elkins, West Virginia.

Some streets in the area were named for the developers, some for the states, and others were numbered, such as First Avenue, now West John Street extended; and Second, Third, Fourth, and Fifth avenues, all running eastward off Winchester Avenue. There are Baker, Berry, Bowers, Buxton and Wilson streets and

Faulkner, Maryland, New York, Virginia and West Virginia avenues and some I might have missed. We must remember, this section of Martinsburg was still quite rural. The only school was the Mason School, which sat on a hill at the point formed where Maryland and Faulkner avenues join at the beginning of what is now the 800 block.

Fern vividly remembered her early days at the Mason School where she started when she was only four years old. "This was the school then," she said, showing a picture she had drawn several years later. "We outgrew the first story, then they built the second story, and the older grades went upstairs. It must have been about 1900 or 1901 when I started because I'm 84 now. Miss Nancy Showers was my first teacher. I don't remember that—I was so little—but one time I went in the W. O. Nicklas Furniture Store to buy something. She was the secretary there, and she said, 'Do you know I was your very first school teacher?' I said, 'No, I thought Miss Laura Tabler was.'"

Fern remembered that when they came into the room early in the morning and it wasn't warm yet, Miss Laura would say, "We'll sing."

"We'd all stand up and sing," she smiled, "and that would warm us all up. By that time the fire would be burning pretty good. Then sometime during the day—you know how it is with a bunch of school kids, the air gets pretty stale—she'd say, 'One of you big boys get by each window and we'll stand and sing and we'll open the windows.'"

Other teachers at the Mason School were Jim Snyder, father of Joseph C. Snyder, a local banker; and "Mose" Cole, later a funeral director, Fern recalled.

I remember my husband Max saying that he and his brother Bob attended Mason School at one time. They lived on Georgia Avenue and that also was rural. I don't know who his teacher was. Willis Evans was superintendent of Berkeley County Schools at the time of Fern's story. (There also was a superintendent of city schools.) It was Superintendent Evans who signed her diploma when she graduated from the 10th grade. She still had her test papers at the time of our interview.

"I couldn't take that examination now! My soul! I think I made 96. Mr. Charlie Gain was my last teacher. Another school superintendent was Mr. Eddie Tabler."

The second house, built next door, provided two more schoolrooms, one upstairs and one down. It was on the second floor of this second house that St. Luke's United Methodist church had its beginning as the Second United Brethren Church, a mission church of the First United Brethren. The latter church, then located on Pennsylvania Avenue one block off North Queen, was replaced in 1912 by the one at 549 North Queen, and following several mergers, became known as Otterbein United Methodist Church.

The "Boom" area continued to grow, attracting residential and industrial development beyond its founders' wildest dreams and becoming the gateway to both Route 11 South and Route 9 East from Martinsburg.

Mason School's population continued to grow, and when it outgrew the four rooms in the two buildings, the house across the street was rented for expansion, providing four more rooms.

"When they outgrew those, that's when they built Winchester Avenue School. I was married and living in Virginia by that time," Fern said wistfully, "and I never got to enjoy that. But it's been a wonderful school. They've had good teachers."

A short tour of the neighborhood around the former school

reveals the fact that the buildings that housed Mason School have become handsome homes. The area is completely built up now.

Fern turned and pointed eastward.

"Away over there was a little, hard-looking house they moved out there on wheels" she said, "and that was a great curiosity, you know. That was what they used to call the 'pest house.' They took people there who had smallpox and whoever was going to stay with them. They were quarantined and they stayed in that little building. We could stand out here on our porch and see it, because this was all open country. It wasn't drained very well, and there were ponds you could skate on and everything."

The "Boom" area continued to grow, attracting residential and industrial development beyond its founders' wildest dreams and becoming the gateway to both Route 11 South and Route 9 East from Martinsburg.

This then is the history of the "Boom," where electricity was first turned on January 6, 1911, a fact carried many years in the annals of *The Journal.*

Remember Sunday Company?

Adapted from ***The Journal***
August 6, 2000

Remember when company came visiting on Sunday afternoons? I can remember when the casual invitation, "Come out to see us!" resulted in just that—a ring of the doorbell, a glad, "Well, look who's here! Come in!" and an afternoon of conversation with friends.

Could it be that television helped to kill that wonderful custom? It might have been a contributing factor, but I believe that "company" went out of style even earlier, and planned parties came in.

Those afternoons probably sound quite tame to today's youngsters. We never played ball or prisoner's base or hide-and-seek, or even Old Maid or Flinch on Sunday. Activities were limited due to the sacredness of the day. We came home from church, took off hat and gloves, put on an apron, and dished up dinner. My father asked the blessing and we ate until we couldn't take another bite. Then we spent the day in quiet activities.

If company came to our house, I sat on the porch swing and answered questions put to me by visiting relatives and friends about my school grades and listened to stories about my parents when they were "young ones," or the "goings-on" in Martinsburg in years past.

Those discussions were interesting and filled with information which would have made me a walking history book if my mind could have held the bits of local history. Unfortunately, much of it is lost because I just couldn't retain it all.

Later, at a nod from Mother, I'd follow her into the kitchen and help get out the best china plates and carry slices of homemade cake and glasses of iced tea out to the cool porch. Then would follow more good-natured talk and laughter and compliments about my mother's baking.

Before leaving for home, if it was a long walk or drive, guests would go down the brick walk under the grape arbor to the little building behind the wisteria trellis. On the way, my mother garnered more compliments concerning her flowers and the vegetable gardens, her special joy. If the season was right, they carried sacks of these goodies home with them.

After they departed, we stood at the gate to wave as they rounded the corner at Hooge Street School, then we headed to

Photo from author's collection

A favorite Sunday pastime of yesteryear was afternoon visiting with friends and relatives. In this photo, a young Ethel, in white hat with back to camera, chats on the porch during a visit with relatives in Waynesboro, Pennsylvania, in the 1920s.

the kitchen to wash the dishes. Hot water was poured from the steaming kettle on the stove into the granite dishpan and cooled a bit with water from the pitcher pump. The cake of Octagon soap was rubbed into the dishcloth and the cleanup followed.

The kitchen sink was also the lavatory. A granite washbasin hung beneath, and the bath was taken before the sink while fresh clothes warmed on the oven door if the weather was chilly.

The medicine cabinet, where shaving supplies and other toiletries were kept, hung on the wall over the sink. Under the cabinet was an elaborately decorated tin case holding an assortment of combs and brushes, hairpins and a safety pin or two. Another shelf convenient to the sink had hooks underneath to hold the blue granite cups in several sizes, handy for drinking. On the shelf was the salt crock, where salt was always measured by the pinch. Another shelf with a bright ruffled skirt held the kitchen clock, and a metal matchbox beside the Oriole gas range provided wooden matches. In the hottest weather, a piece of linoleum floor covering cut to size was placed over the cook stove, and it became a work table while cooking activities were transferred to the gas range. No one considered using the gas range at any other time in those early days, for its quarter meter in the basement was fed only when the heat from the cook stove would be unbearable. The gas range was considered the height of luxury.

On the center panel of the outside door was a nail where the "huck-type" (rough fabric) kitchen towel hung by a loop. A rack on the wall behind the stove held the tea towels. These were also homemade, of course, from the ever-available muslin flour sacks. They were nothing like the much-too-small tea towels of today, but were ample in size so that they could be wrapped around the dishes, pots and pans.

Dominating the room was the Hoosier kitchen cabinet, that large, golden oak piece with just about everything needed for cooking and baking, even to the heavy, pull-out enameled table-top for rolling out dough for pies and dumplings. This kitchen cabinet and the Singer Sewing Machine in the dining room were my mother's most prized possessions. It was in this setting that we washed the company dishes and put them away, while we talked over the unexpected visit we had enjoyed so much.

This was the magic of company in the days before visiting became such a planned event, and before life became so complicated that we had little time for living.

Wouldn't it be nice to start dropping in again?

And while we're reminiscing, let's look at a few more of our memories. Modern living is lots of fun and much more convenient than in the past. We wouldn't go back, even if we could, but in many ways, life today is a mixed blessing. It seems to have dulled our senses to the little things that once were so precious.

Years ago, we went to sleep to the chirp of a cricket outside the window and woke to the happy song of birds. We traded these small pleasures for the comfort of air-conditioning and try to convince ourselves that its hum is just as pleasing.

We stay in our homes all day long, with the windows tightly closed and live with the sound of this same air-conditioning, along with the hum of the refrigerator, the music on the stereo and the rhythm of the washing machine, the dryer, and the dishwasher. And don't forget the grind and splash of the disposal unit, and the whirring sounds of the vacuum cleaner and the floor polisher.

Comfortable and convenient, to be sure. Work-saving as well. But where are the familiar sounds we once knew?

Where is the cheery "Yoo hoo!" of a neighbor at the back fence waiting to show her daughter's new dress she has just finished for Easter? Or the song of a mother at the sink or the ironing board? One of the most comforting sounds I remember hearing as a child upon waking in the morning was my mother humming at the ironing board, and now and then a soft click as she set the iron aside.

We now have refrigerators that dispense fresh ice cubes, so our youngsters will never know the thrill of being handed a dripping piece of ice (free!) by the iceman on a hot summer day. I can still feel the icy water dripping onto my bare feet! The iceman drove his truck from door to door, stopping wherever the ice card hung in the window or on the porch post.

Remember the ice card? It was a very necessary part of our time. It hung diagonally from a hole in the corner, depending upon whether you wanted 25, 50, 75, or 100 pounds of ice, and the iceman knew at a glance where to start skillfully cutting with his sharp ice pick. You bought the size that would fit the top of your refrigerator and, more often than not, the lid wouldn't close tightly the first day because the ice stuck up too high and was then covered with papers to help keep the cold in.

Our refrigerator was popular because it had a water tank in one side and a spigot on the front. Above the spigot hung a small swinging bracket with a small metal cup. All who wanted a drink helped themselves. My little friends loved it.

We also had a very unusual service—a meat man named Gantt Miller. He stopped his truck at a central point on our block, picked up his bugle and played a rousing "Reveille," or, as we called it, "You can't get 'em up!" Well, it got 'em up! The sound brought bonneted women out of their houses, wiping hands on their aprons, ready to see what values he had that morning. This was an important part of the day. The ladies made their purchases from the meats he had hanging in his truck, then lingered to discuss community news or compare notes on plans for dinner.

Brief encounters such as these were important in the neighborhood, for they linked the women together during a time when there were few telephones, and personal contacts were necessary for friendship to take root and flourish.

Yes, many of the very things that make life so much easier now are indeed mixed blessings, aren't they?

And, by the way, drop in sometime. We'd love to have you!

Wheels Played a Part in My Life

Adapted from ***The Journal***
February 23, 2003

Wheels have always been an important part of my life. I never learned to roller skate and couldn't ride a bike, and my earliest memories of the automobile are rather limited. We didn't have a car at home and, frankly, there were only a couple on the street where I grew up. I was born in Martinsburg in 1915, and there probably weren't too many cars in town at that time.

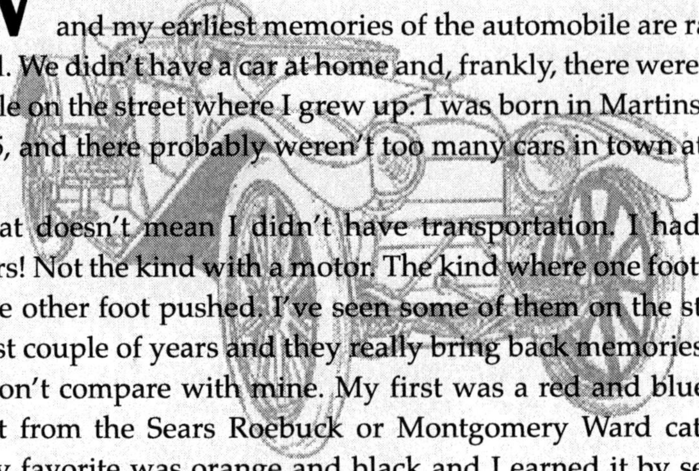

That doesn't mean I didn't have transportation. I had two scooters! Not the kind with a motor. The kind where one foot rode and the other foot pushed. I've seen some of them on the streets the past couple of years and they really bring back memories. But they don't compare with mine. My first was a red and blue one bought from the Sears Roebuck or Montgomery Ward catalog. But my favorite was orange and black and I earned it by selling subscriptions to the Harrisburg Telegraph. I loved it, and proud were the days I rode down the long hill through the North Queen Street subway, with the wind blowing through my hair. That was a real thrill!

But I'll tell you about some cars I do remember. Some of my out-of-town relatives came to visit in their automobiles. Uncle Will and Aunt Sarah came from York, Pennsylvania, in their Buick, and Uncle Charlie came from Berkeley Springs in his Willys Knight. Both of those were wide open touring cars, of course, with the side curtains they put on in case of rain. In cold weather they carried blankets to keep warm. There were no heaters, of course.

Speaking of Berkeley Springs, that reminds me. My Aunt Emma took in boarders. You don't hear of that often any more, do you? One of her boarders had a car—I guess you could call it that, but I have no idea what kind it was. There was just a chassis with a metal seat for two in front and a gas tank right behind the back seat. Aunt Emma and my cousin Hazel rode on the front seat with the driver, and my mother and I rode in the back.

Now the road to Berkeley Springs wasn't paved. I remember it was very rough, and more like clay and ashes. There was no shoulder, of course. The vehicle didn't have much power. When we came to a hill, we had to get out and walk, and Bill chugged up to the top of the hill and stopped to let us get in and ride to the next hill. Aunt Emma was short and very stout. She was always out of breath when we got to the top. You know how many hills there are between Martinsburg and Berkeley Springs? A lot!! A trip up and back with a short visit was a day's journey. So it didn't happen often.

My cousin George stayed with us for a short time after my Aunt Nell died, and while he was there he bought a brand new shiny black Model T Ford. That was about 1922 or 1923. I guess I rode in it a couple times, but the time I really remember was when he took us over the mountain to see where a bootlegger had shot an officer. I don't remember the story, but I think the Feds cornered him in a barn and got him. Crime was something rare around here in those days, and everybody wanted to go over to see where it had happened. They talked about it for months.

Then I remember hearing my dad's Aunt Laura Brown, in Williamsport, tell about her grandson taking her for her first automobile ride. When they got back to the house, they both came in laughing. He told the family his brakes hadn't held when he pulled up, and he ran into the fence post. He said he was a little shaken up and asked Grandma if she was scared. Aunt Laura laughed and said, " I thought that was the way he had to stop the thing!"

I didn't drive a car when Max and I were married. He tried to teach me lots of times, but it always ended up with my stopping the car, getting out, and saying, "All right! You drive." My sister-in-law Jane finally convinced me I needed to drive, and she taught me. But I didn't have an auto of my own until my daughter Sharilyn started in the first grade at Burke Street School. There was no bus service for town students and we parents car-pooled our kids to school. So I had to have a car.

That was 1953. Max bought me a 1939 Model A Ford. I was happy as a lark. I had a car and could take my turn in the car pool. Then one day when it was time for school to let out, it started to rain. I drove down and parked on Raleigh Street to wait. Suddenly, I realized it was raining inside as well as outside. The kids came running, jumped in, breathed a sigh of relief, then threw their coats over their heads to keep dry. I tried to start the car. No such luck. It wouldn't move. Drowned out.

Sharilyn went back into the school and asked Ted Matthews, the principal, to call Mo Keiter's filling station for help. Mo came down and got us started. Not long after that, we drove to Washington and got a 1957 Plymouth. It ran out of gas on the way home because the gas gauge was faulty, but I don't remember having any other problems with that one.

Max loved cars and traded every two or three years—not for new cars but used ones in good condition—until our later years. We had a good many during our 62 years of marriage. There were Plymouths, Chevrolets, Pontiacs, a Subaru, Fords, Hondas, a Cadillac, even a couple of used Mercedes. His favorite used car salesman, Frank Corbin, was always on the lookout for a good buy for him. But our last two were new Dodge Caravans he bought from Buzz Poland, the last one a 1996 that I'm still driving. Buzz, of course, is the owner of Union Sales, a garage and dealership his grandfather, Bonn Poland, opened in 1913.

Max was a good automobile mechanic. His father, N. L. Bovey, owned The Shenandoah Garage on the corner of Winchester Avenue and King Street and later teamed up with Lloyd Janes. Max learned a lot when he hung around the auto repair business with those two. Bovey and Janes were well known auto mechanics in Martinsburg many years ago. I ran across one of their advertising cards once. It read, "You wreck 'em—We fix 'em. Bovey & Janes." Max worked at many occupations, but he never lost his interest in auto repair. He worked with Burney Branham and Allen Hendricks at Bryant Snapp's Garage on North Queen Street for some time. Later, he worked on heavy equipment for Potomac Construction, and his last work was on maintenance of equipment for Capitol Cement, later Martin-Marietta Corporation, until he retired in 1977.

After we were married, he worked at various types of jobs, but after regular working hours he did auto and bike repair and sold Whizzer motors for bicycles. That was in the 1940s. Many times he came home from work to find a young fellow waiting at the curb for him to take a look at his bike or order him a Whizzer motor and mount it on his bike.

One of the best known and most highly respected garages in town was that of Trammell Hollis on Winchester Avenue. Max worked there for a while too, mainly as a grease monkey. Trammell Hollis was the Chevrolet dealer and did a fine business. Then there was Kershner's Garage on West King Street at the cor-

Winchester Telephone C. & P. Telephone

The Shenandoah Garage

N. L. BOVEY, Proprietor

Automobile Accessories **Studebaker Automobiles**

Repairing a Specialty

Corner Winchester Avenue and King Street

MARTINSBURG, - - - W. VA.

ner of College. There were others, I'm sure, but I don't recall too much about them.

There were a good many service stations—not filling stations, but service stations. You drove in and a man in uniform hustled over and asked if he could help you. He filled the gas tank, and busied himself cleaning your windshield and side windows too if they needed it. He or someone else at the station would check out any small problem he noticed or one you mentioned when you drove in. He'd check your anti-freeze and your oil and make an appointment to change your oil at the first opportunity. You knew you were in good hands.

Some of these stations were run by Firestone, Johnny Spickler, Bob Barbour, Bryant Snapp, Mo Keiter. . . . I'm sure you could add to the list, for there were many of them.

I know the Norwalk Underslung automobile was manufactured in Martinsburg from 1912 to 1922. I don't remember anything about it, but my dad and Max both talked about it and were proud that it had been manufactured here.

There's an enthusiastic group of local people who are keeping the name of the Norwalk alive through the years—the Norwalk Antique Car Club. The club has an interesting history, and it's about to mark its 21st anniversary in June of this year. Garry Murphy, club historian, filled me in on its background.

The nucleus of the club was a group that first met June 1, 1982, at the home of Howard and Marge York at The Woods to discuss organizing. In that first group, in addition to the Yorks, were Garry and Darla Murphy, Buck and Junella Sigler, Jerry Cogle, Paul Cogle, Sr., Paul Cogle, Jr., Harry Hudson, and Buck Chaney.

The Yorks, the Cogles, the Murphys, and Hudson had a picnic at The Woods in July, but no serious action was taken until October, when Jimmy Porterfield arranged for them to meet in a room at the Central Fire Station in Martinsburg. In the first step toward organization, Paul Cogle, Jr., Hudson, and Ed Morgan of

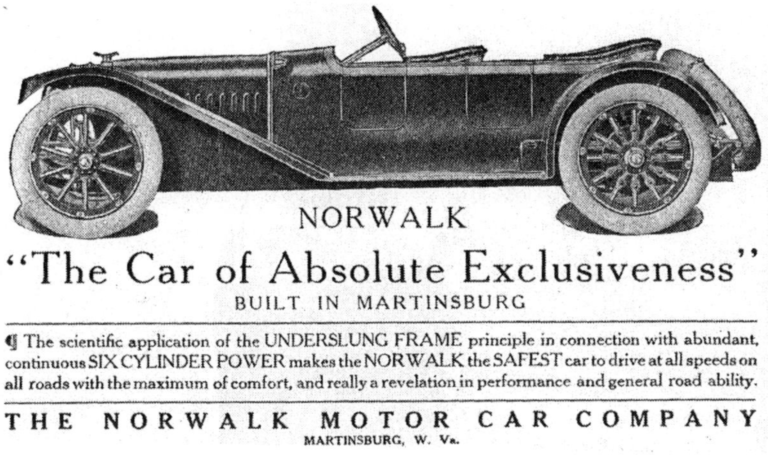

This 1914 advertisement for the Norwalk touts the car's "underslung frame" and "six cylinder power." The car was manufactured by the Norwalk Motor Car Company of Martinsburg.

Charles Town, were named to a nominating committee.

The question of naming the club came next. Suggestions included Gateway Touring Society, Norwalk Tri-County Antique Auto Club, and the BJM (for Berkeley, Jefferson, Morgan) Antique Auto Club. By majority vote, the winner was Norwalk Antique Car Club.

Several members belonged to other clubs that were affiliated with Antique Automobile Clubs of America. However, the fledgling club wanted to be independent and draw up and adopt its own stated purpose and bylaws.

On October 16, 1982, the first officers were elected to hold office through 1983. They were Garry Murphy, president; Jimmy Porterfield, vice president; Martin Frye, secretary; Ray Miller, treasurer; and Howard York, activities chairman.

Bylaws were formed and specified that a member must be a resident of Berkeley, Jefferson or Morgan County. An officers' term of office is November to November. The Intent and Purpose of the Club: "The preservation and restoration of antique and special interest vehicles and related antiques, and to provide technical information and activities for the mutual enjoyment of members." There were 45 members when officers were installed November 27, 1982, at Henry's Country Inn in Jefferson County.

The first Christmas party was held at the home of Bob Poland and well attended. It was decided that the club would meet on the second Thursday of each month. Darla Murphy became editor of the club newsletter and served 16 years.

Twenty of their faithful members have been lost by death through the years, but the club has grown and now boasts 145 members. Officers for 2003 are: John Clevenger, president; Ron Butts, vice president; Garry Murphy, secretary; Harry Hudson, treasurer; and Janie Butts, activities chairperson. Kevin Carter, Max Mosse, and Denis Foley are board-members-at-large. Betty Hutzler is editor of the newsletter.

The club now has monthly dinner meetings and big summer picnics, and gets together for a tour or two each year. Since 1998, the Norwalk Antique Car Club's auto show has been a popular feature of the Mountain State Apple Harvest Festival.

It's great that this group is keeping alive such an important part of local history. We congratulate them on their foresight. Would that more efforts were being made toward preservation of Martinsburg's industrial history.

Our Early Culture

Our Cultural Past

Martinsburg offered a direct ticket to Hollywood

Adapted from ***The Journal***
January 15, 2000

Martinsburg citizens have always been culture-conscious. Despite setbacks and problems, they have worked through the years, with varying degrees of success, to bring cultural opportunities to this community.

Some years ago, I raised a question concerning this topic while visiting the late William C. Schneider. Mr. Schneider was well known as office and credit manager for Emmert's, a downtown department store for many years. He was a recognized source of information concerning local history and had a remarkable memory. He provided many interesting facts on the subject of the city's early culture, and I shall draw from notes I took that day in this story.

I might point out that the folks mentioned in his recollections are all gone now; thus I will not insert "the late" before their names.

The Theatorium, a moving picture theater, was operated by a W. H. Crawford on North Queen Street across from Martinsburg City Hall in a site now owned by the Veterans of Foreign Wars. The theater moved to the building on West King Street that was later occupied by the Sally Shop and is now the home of *The Journal's* circulation department. In the summer, the backyard was used as an outdoor theater. Still later, the theater moved across the street. I have no information as to when it closed.

The old Central Opera House was on the corner of North Queen and West Martin streets, next door to the Hammann plumbing shop. Mr. Schneider said many fine companies appeared there. This opera house was remembered fondly by my dad and his cronies. Walter H. Lambert was the owner of the building, and his brother, Andrew, was theater manager in 1905. The building was destroyed by fire in 1919.

The Dreamland Theater opened its doors about 1908 on the corner of Queen and Burke streets, across from the Market House, now the home of Market House Restaurant. Louis Harley, brother of Dudley Harley, local banker at the time, was one of its first managers. The venture was short-lived, however, closing in about two years.

Youngsters will be interested in knowing that in 1906 Martinsburg had a roller skating rink on South Queen Street, at the present location of the Boys and Girls Club. It was in opera-

Photo courtesy Berkeley County Historical Society

The Central Opera House, shown at far right, was one of several theaters contributing to Martinsburg's early culture. Erected at the corner of Queen and Martin streets in 1902, the building was destroyed by fire in 1919.

tion about three years, until the Empire Theatre opened on the site. Capital for this theater came from Winchester, Virginia, and the first manager was a Mr. Hunter. This also proved to be a short-lived venture, however, for it closed about 1910.

The Strand Theater, operated by Bill Horsfall and his sister, was built on North Queen Street on ground once used as a hitching yard by the Valley Hotel next door. Valley Hotel later became the Washington Hotel and operated for many years, until it was razed in 1967. Martinsburg City Hall now occupies the site.

At one time there was a theater in the present location of Christopher's Restaurant on South Queen Street, across from Patterson's Drug Store. "Tiny" Boyd, a man weighing about 300 pounds, was pianist there for a time. He was followed by Mary Comrey Rouark. I don't know the name of that theater, but Mr. Schneider recalled that on opening night everyone present received a big red rose.

Still another theater operated for a time on the lot on North Queen Street now used as a display lot for Union Sales Company. This was an open-air theater leased for the summer by a Washington company and managed by a man named Willis. It closed as a movie theater in October 1912, but was used later by Governor Henry D. Hatfield and Abe Lilly for campaign rallies.

The Central Theatre on East Burke Street was built about 1922 by M. A. Little. One of the first managers was A. C. Irons. It featured westerns and "B" movies for the most part. That theater was razed to make way for city parking facilities.

During the early years, remember, all of the films were black and white and silent. Realistic sound was provided by nimble fingers at a piano or pump organ, stationed in a box where the player could see the screen. Appropriate music was effective in bringing the films to life. Soft, romantic music accompanied the love scenes, the Wedding March was played during wedding scenes, and funeral dirges brought out the handkerchiefs of viewers for serious illness or death scenes.

Most exciting of all were the sounds produced for the Western films. Here the piano or organ was played with increasing volume so that you would believe the realism of the chases, wagon wheels, gun battles or fistfights. It took no imagination to hear the hoof beats of the horses, the gunshots, or the sound of flesh striking flesh.

To my recollection, *The Jazz Singer* with Al Jolson, produced in 1927, was the first movie with sound. Maxine Newbraugh of Berkeley Springs, longtime writer for *The Journal*, tells me the first one she remembers seeing was *Uncle Tom's Cabin* in Martinsburg when she was about six years old.

After the advent of sound came the musicals, such as *Lullaby of Broadway, 42nd Street* and others, bringing an all new assortment of talent, vocalists, dancers and musicians: Jeannette MacDonald and Nelson Eddy, Fred Astaire and Ginger Rogers, Ruby Keeler, Deanna Durbin, and others. The rough and tumble cowboys of an earlier era were joined by the singing cowboys, such as Roy Rogers and Gene Autry.

The State Theatre was the last to be operated in the city, and this too was short-lived, lasting only a few years. It was located across the street from the Sally Shop, on West King Street.

The Apollo, Martinsburg's only remaining original theater, was built about 1913 by the H. P. Thorn family, with C. E. Kent as architect. Miss Alice Shoemaker operated a dance studio upstairs. This theater is undergoing continuing renovation and is enjoying a renaissance as a popular spot for theatergoers, under the able management of the Apollo Civic Theatre Association.

The association, headed by Dr. Dale Herman, president, sponsors live shows, and has brought out some remarkable area talent, coached by prominent directors. It also sponsors an annual children's summer theater workshop, followed by an excellent presentation by the children. This group's work is a most commendable addition to the cultural life of the community, and is very well received.

During the years of the Depression, a 15- or 25-cent ticket to the movies lifted us out of the world we knew into the world of fantasy created by Hollywood.

Movie houses abound in the shopping areas outside the city proper, but I wonder if they play to the packed houses the earlier ones knew. Lines of eager customers regularly reached for blocks as people waited impatiently for admittance.

During the years of the Depression, a 15- or 25-cent ticket to the movies lifted us out of the world we knew into the world of fantasy created by Hollywood. There, the sirens such as Joan Crawford, Bette Davis, Myrna Loy, Hedy Lamarr, Marlene Dietrich, and others, wore their sleek satins and velvets, their minks, their four-inch heels, and their finger-waved hair with its spit curls. They carried long cigarette holders and champagne glasses as they rolled mascaraed eyes and sought to steal the affections of the handsome leading men—Robert Taylor, Clark Gable, John Payne, Gary Cooper, Jimmy Stewart, and others—away from the sweet and loyal hometown girl in her little print dress and her Cuban-heeled sandals. Sometimes they succeeded, but usually at the end, the hero returned to shy Mary Pickford, Debbie Reynolds, Ruby Keeler, Sylvia Sidney, Claudette Colbert or one of the other nice girls, accompanied by the sighs of the girls in the audience. This was the Apollo.

The story was a bit different at the Central and the Strand. There the audiences were mainly of the male gender, young, loud, sometimes boisterous, as they watched Tom Mix, Rex Allen, Hopalong Cassidy, or other cowboy heroes in their white hats swing fists at the bad guys in their black hats, or let 'em have it with their six-shooters or rifles.

Magically, the music would produce the needed effects, rising in a crescendo to almost shake the room. Excited young voices would shout "Get 'im!" or "Look out!" to warn the hero of impending danger and groan or clap when fist met flesh, depending upon whether it was the hero or the villain being slugged.

Youngsters could pay their five or 10 cents and spend the whole afternoon, their hearts racing again and again at the cliff-hanger ending of the popular serials. They knew they'd have to come back the next Saturday to see how their hero got out of his predicament.

Some of the would-be tough guys wore cowboy outfits with boots and chaps or outfits assembled from play clothing available and carried a popgun, a stick, or other makeshift weapon. Of course, they couldn't pack their guns in the theater. I might add that what was violence to that generation was quite tame compared to what today's youngsters can see on the screen in their own homes.

On the other hand, mothers wanted their little girls to be Shirley Temple. They put their little darlings' locks on rollers to dry, then carefully wrapped the curls around their fingers to copy the effect achieved by the child star's hairdresser. Shirley Temple perms were popular. The little ones tried to tap dance like their idol, and many succeeded.

The culture of our time has a tremendous influence upon us, beginning in our youth and continuing throughout our lives. We have to be proud of the efforts of our citizens through the years to provide opportunities for our cultural enrichment.

The Apollo Theatre

Revitalized for a new generation

Adapted from ***The Journal***
October 15, 2000

I'm sure Harry P. Thorn, visionary builder and founder of Thorn Lumber Company, would be delighted to know the Apollo Theatre he built in 1913 has been reborn and revitalized for yet another generation.

It's about time to take a new look at the historic theater and its importance in Martinsburg's culture through the years. I'll borrow liberally from a favorite story, then bring you up to date.

According to Nell Thorn Baynham, daughter of the builder, her father hired Reginald Geare, well-known Washington theater architect, who later designed the Knickerbocker Theater in New York City, to do the interior, and Chappy Kent the exterior.

On the first floor, silent movies were shown during the '20s, accompanied at first by appropriate music by Mary O'Rourke at the piano and later, after a large investment in a Mohler Organ, by the music and sound effects it produced.

In the '20s and '30s the Kiwanis Club, under the direction of Albert Geyer, staged variety and minstrel shows.

Through the '30s, '40s, and '50s, young people packed the seats on Saturday afternoons for talking movies, newsreels, and comedies, and there were occasional amateur productions by local talent. Offerings varied through the years, but the Apollo was always a popular spot.

Traveling vaudeville shows played at the Apollo, including performers such as Will Rogers, cowboy Tex Ritter, and the famous Rubinoff with his Stradivarius violin.

The first to bring local theater to the community was the Berkeley County Civic Theatre (BCCT). In its 1936–37 season, it presented a one-act play each month, plus three major productions annually in the Martinsburg High School auditorium. World War II interrupted, but in 1971 the group was revived. In 1973, the BCCT vowed to renovate the theater and present the first musical production at the Apollo. *Oklahoma* played to a standing room only audience and was followed by other musicals and plays.

Early in the Apollo's history, the second and third floors were the scene of varied activities, such as card parties with 10 or 15 tables, a stylish entertainment of the time; Martinsburg Business College; fire company bazaars and fairs, and dancing lessons at Miss Alice Shoemaker's Dance School. It was also the site of Roy Harrison's satellite WJEJ radio station.

Chief among this writer's memories are the dances at Roseland Ballroom on the second floor. Here, in a romantic garden setting of white-painted latticework entwined with roses, some of the finest musical aggregations available performed to the delight of the public.

Here, young men in dark jackets, bow ties and white flannels whirled, twirled, and "dipped" their ladies, dressed in their finest chiffon, shantung, or eyelet dresses, their red lips painted in a cupid's bow, hair brushed into deep finger waves, and Cuban-heeled sandals clicking a staccato on the mirror-like floor.

Magic was created by the crystal ball overhead reflecting rainbow colors from spotlights in the corners of the room. The ball revolved slowly with the waltz and faster and faster with the quick rhythm of the fox trot until the young dancers sank down breathless upon the nearest chair at the end of the number.

Who provided the music for these evenings? Chief among

them were Jack Schill and his West Virginians and Roy Harrison and his Rosemont Park Orchestra. Harrison was manager of the ballroom and Rosemont park, the latter being the predecessor of the present War Memorial Park on North Tennessee Avenue.

The ball revolved slowly with the waltz and faster and faster with the quick rhythm of the fox trot until the young dancers sank down breathless upon the nearest chair at the end of the number.

Members of the orchestra were Harrison himself, director and violinist; Wallace Reynolds, vocalist; Harry Hale, William Crawford, Nelson Hicks, Howard Fellers, Leonard Fulk, Andy Oliver, Yeakley Brown, Bill McBride, and Homer Johnson.

One of the favorite waltzes of the day was "Beautiful Shenandoah Valley," a ballad by M. H. Rouark, general manager of Shenandoah Valley Attractions, which booked bands for Roseland. For local audiences at least, it took its place right up there with Strauss's "Blue Danube."

Dan Gregory and his orchestra of 13 artists played for the Kiwanis Charity Ball at Roseland, a benefit, or, as fliers announced, "Christmas Cheer for Under-privileged Children, offering dancing from 9:30 until 2, chaperoned, and all for 50 cents admission." This was Thursday, December 21, 1934.

Booked for the 11th Annual Flapper's Ball on Monday, January 15, 1935, was Red Bailey, the Joy Boy himself, and his orchestra, "twelve musical doctors, modern rhythm specialists," with dancing from 9 until 2, admission at $1.50 per couple.

Photo courtesy Berkeley County Historical Society

The Apollo Theatre, built in 1913 by Harry P. Thorn, has been the setting through the years for movies, traveling vaudeville and minstrel shows, local theater, big-name entertainment, and social events. The historic structure has undergone multiple and extensive renovations in its lifetime.

Appearing on the same program was the Cheer girl of the South, Merry Virginia, "who makes a piano talk when she sings."

Don't let those admission prices fool you—that $1.50 represented a full day's wages for many of the dancers.

Advertised as "West Virginia's most popular ballroom," Roseland has a place in the memories of many who called Martinsburg and the Shenandoah Valley home, and was, indeed, as the fliers claimed: "The joy spot of Martinsburg."

Fred Waring and the Pennsylvanians graced the stage of the Apollo in 1926, it is recalled, but local promoters were never successful in getting that talent upstairs.

Renovations in recent years have included a new roof on the building, replacement of many of the windows, addition of a fire alarm sprinkler system, and a second flight of stairs. The orchestra pit was reopened after being covered in 1951. Theater seats have been replaced and space has been provided on the third floor for a costume shop and artist's studio.

The Apollo Theatre is frequently rented out for organizations and events such as country western style dances, scholarship pageants, and ballet recitals, and has been the site of performances of the West Virginia Symphony Orchestra.

The Apollo Civic Theatre company itself produces five main-stage shows annually, as well as dinner/dessert theater and audience-participation murder mysteries. A summer theater workshop offers an opportunity for young people, eight to 18, to perform to the delight of the community.

Headed by Dale S. Herman, president, the Apollo Civic Theatre Board of Directors states its goal is to make the theater a community gathering place where all are welcome.

Other officers are: Kathy Best, vice president; Drew Catrow, recording secretary; Bess Daniels, treasurer; Tom Hutchcraft; technical vice president; Tami McDonald, artistic vice president, and Harriett Eyler, corresponding secretary.

Wonder if the crystal ball will ever be polished up to create its magic again? I hope so. It certainly brought happiness to those young people who grew up in the Great Depression and to whom it spelled real luxury and a taste of the truly finer things in life.

Hotel Shenandoah

Now known as the Gateway Inn

Adapted from ***The Journal***

Hotel Shenandoah was situated on the corner of North Queen and West Martin streets. I'll quote Wilmore Basey, a longtime employee and a walking encyclopedia in regards to the hotel. It was built in 1924 by the American Hotel Chain and received its name from a contest in which citizens entered their suggestions. The "Shenandoah" entry was so popular that the prize was broken down to a minimal amount shared by many winners.

Prices were very different from those of today. The best room available, a double room with television (later) and bath with shower was $3.50. A more modest room with commode and washbowl was $1.50.

Basey worked for hotel managers Tom Martin, Bill Standley, Dan Frankenberry, B. A. Poland and Fran Bradt. Standley stayed 11 years, then returned to make his home here after retirement. The Bradts also remained here.

"I've seen a lot of things go on around here. This was a beautiful place and the only place in town where people could come and have a good time," mused Basey. A faraway look came into his eyes as he visually scanned the lobby of the former Shenandoah, once recognized as one of the top hotels in the Shenandoah Valley.

"I came to work here in 1936," he told me. "But I'd been in

hotel business since I was 14-years-old, when I used to go and help my father at the Berkeley Hotel. He was head bellman there."

The Berkeley Hotel on West King Street was razed years before to make way for the Citizens National Bank (which later became One Valley Bank) on that site, a property now a part of the Berkeley County Courthouse. As a teenager, young Wilmore had often gone there and stayed all day to be of assistance wherever he was needed.

"In those days it wasn't a question whether you worked or not—you worked," he said. "Whenever anybody asked my father if he knew where he could get somebody to work—he never said no. He got one of his five boys. And we went. We cleaned, or we did whatever the job was."

So when a handicapped guest needed someone to help him out of bed to eat his dinner, Basey was the one to do it. He was there to help him back into bed too. Each time, he received a dime. "I hung around there all day for 20 cents," he smiled. "But with 20 cents I could go to a movie for 10 cents, buy a coke for a nickel, and still have a nickel left."

Clerks at the Berkeley Hotel during that time were Bobby Brumbaugh and Bob Butler. (Brumbaugh told me recently that he

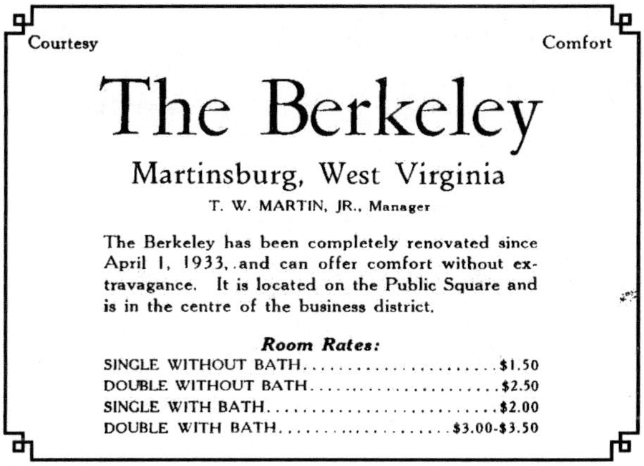

went from the Berkeley to the Shenandoah and worked there 22 years.)

Basey turned back to his stories about the Shenandoah. "Before I came here to work, I used to play here every Saturday night with the West Virginia Troubadors," he recalled. "We played here from 4 to 7 in the evening then went on to Roseland Ballroom on the third floor over the Apollo and played there from 9 to 12."

Basey was the entertainer, singing and dancing with the band. Clyde Harris was director and George Jones arranged the music. Other band members were a Mr. Scarboro and George Jones, who played violin; Sam Nash, drums; Norman Jones, saxophone; Grant Arnent, bass viola; Harold Ford and Braxton Reed, trumpets.

Basey remembers when the Horticultural Society had its banquets at the hotel and 350 to 500 people were served. "I was in charge of banquets," he said with pride.

He told of catering a party for the Interwoven Stocking

In The Shenandoah Valley

THE HOTEL
SHENANDOAH

New -- Modern -- Fireproof
European Plan

FREE PARKING, also GARAGE SERVICE

Excellent Cuisine	**Room Rates**
Coffee Shop Prices	**$2 00 Up**

Operated Direction—American Hotels Corporation
STUART E. HOCKENBURY, Mgr.

MARTINSBURG, WEST VA.

Company at the mill every Christmas. "They cleared off the tables they worked on and we took the food in: big trays of turkey and things—and always a big tray of haddock, because there was always somebody who wanted fish. But we never catered for anybody else, just the Interwoven."

During the Apple Blossom Festival in Winchester, five or six bands regularly stayed at the hotel. They were fed in the ballroom and the downstairs assembly room—all the same menu to keep things easier for the staff.

Before the advent of Interstate 81 the hotel was situated right on Route 11 and Route 9, which meant much through traffic stopped there for meals. Thus Wilmore Basey and the staff met many important people quite casually. He told of the day Robert Kennedy stopped by unannounced and spoke extemporaneously to a session of the Chamber of Commerce.

He recalled his pleasure at meeting Debbie Reynolds, in her early years when she spoke to a United Nations banquet in the Gold Room. He said he still prized her autograph. (In my early years at *The Journal* I interviewed Constance Bennett at the U.N. dinner at The Shenandoah.)

Drew Pearson, Frank Church, Raymond Massey, Jay Rockefeller and John Ford were others he met there, as were Congressman Harley Staggers and Senator Jennings Randolph. He said Randolph never failed to stop by and shake hands, even if he wasn't staying at the hotel.

Basey was saddened by the fact that the hotel was no longer used as such, at the time we talked, remembering that many visitors who stopped in for an overnight stay had been so pleased with the friendliness of the people they met while shopping in our downtown area that they would come back again and again—some even returned later for a vacation of a week or two.

New highways have taken a toll on hotels in many towns, the Shenandoah among them. Those along the interstates are much more accessible. When I was growing up, Martinsburg boasted

Photo courtesy Berkeley County Historical Society

Hotel Shenandoah, built in 1924 on the corner of Queen and Martin streets, was a key stopping place in Martinsburg for tourists and dignitaries and a popular spot for locals to come and have a good time. The hotel later became the Gateway Inn.

three busy hotels—the Berkeley Hotel, the Washington Hotel and the Shenandoah—and a number of tourist homes.

Remember the tourist homes? This must have been the birth of today's bed and breakfast. People would just set aside one or more of their spare rooms and make them up for guests, providing all the amenities they could arrange. Next step was to hang out a lighted sign, "Tourists Welcome—Reasonable Rates," then sit back and await the arrival of some weary travelers. Breakfast was usually available upon request. Morning found the tourist rested, refreshed and merrily on his way, and the hostess with dishes, beds and laundry to do and a few extra dollars in her apron pocket.

The Public Library

*Adapted from **The Journal***
April 8, 2001

We never know where the sound of a familiar name will lead, do we? I heard someone say that Mrs. Estelle Sencindiver celebrated her 98th birthday March 27, 1999. That name rang a bell, and I dug into my archives for some information I knew was there.

It's impossible to think of Estelle without thinking of the Martinsburg Public Library, where her bright eyes and cloud of silver white hair were a familiar sight at the desk for 23 years. She started to work there in March, 1956, and retired March 31, 1979. That certainly qualifies her as an important part of our library's distinguished history.

As the wife of the late Attorney Carroll T. Sencindiver, Estelle had busied herself raising three children and doing volunteer work and had never been employed outside her home. But when her husband passed away, she needed something to occupy her time and her mind. Two years later, when Florence Wright resigned as assistant librarian, Estelle decided to apply for the position. She had attended local schools and Martinsburg Business College prior to her marriage.

Her children, Attorney Vance E. Sencindiver, now circuit court judge; Carolyn, now Mrs. Robert Elmer and a retired school teacher, and Gavin D. Sencindiver, director of Social Services in Washington County, Maryland, disapproved of her decision to apply for work, but gave up trying to dissuade her, thinking she'd not get the position anyway because of her age. She was hired at the age of 53. This was a bit unusual, for at that time, few people—particularly women—embarked on their first career that late in life.

At that time, the library boasted 18,000 volumes on its shelves, and occupied four rooms on the second floor of the old Martinsburg City Hall, in the former YMCA on West King

Photo courtesy Berkeley County Historical Society

Before moving to its present location on the Public Square in 1968, the Martinsburg Public Library occupied four rooms on the second floor of the old City Hall building, in the former YMCA on West King Street.

Street. Mrs. Howard Elliott was librarian, Estelle assistant, and Mrs. Geraldine Fitzgerald completed the staff of three. The only new books on the shelves were a rotating supply of about 75, which were sent from Charleston by the West Virginia Library Commission.

"These would soon disappear," Estelle recalled in an interview at the time of her retirement. "Circulation was about 200 a day." She watched it grow to some 800 daily during her tenure. She worked under five librarians, three professional and two non-professional. Mrs. Howard Elliott gave her basic training, and Mrs. George Williams, wife of a doctor at the VA Center, was next. Mrs. Wright later rejoined the staff and she and William McBride worked as secretaries while Estelle handled the desk.

When Mrs. Williams' husband was transferred, Mrs Wright took over as librarian. Mrs. Anna Shewbridge worked during the summer months for two years to direct activities for children. October 1, 1963, Mrs. Wright resigned again and Mr. McBride died shortly thereafter. This left Estelle alone with only pages as assistants from late November until the close of school in 1964, when Mrs. Shewbridge was hired as full-time librarian. It was she who taught Estelle the fine points of genealogical research. Mrs. Shewbridge was succeeded about 10 years later by Peggy Batten.

"When we moved to the new library in 1968, I was given a choice of heading circulation or reference," Estelle said. "I chose reference because it's my first love. I've enjoyed helping a child to seek knowledge, or an adult to seek enjoyment reading or searching family history. While I was helping them, I was learning as I went along. The library has made great strides through the years and I'm confident it will continue to do so under the efficient leadership of Mr. Beall." She referred to the late Campbell Beall, who served many years as chairman of the Berkeley County Library Commission. Her optimistic prediction was to prove true.

Now I'd like to share a bit of the history of the library's humble beginning as I remember it. It was 1926 when I first visited the library, then located on South Maple Avenue just off King Street. It had just opened as the result of much hard work and dedication on the part of the Woman's Club and its first president, Mrs. G. J. E. Sponseller, boosted by financial help from businessmen, industrial corporations and individual citizens.

The shelves could not have been as vast as they appeared to a child's eye, but there I tasted the thrill and excitement of wandering up and down, trying to decide which book I would select as my own for two whole weeks. There was a limit of one book, for supplies were not equal to the demand.

Miss Marion Batchelder was the first librarian, and it was she who filled out my first important and impressive library card—the key to what seemed to be all the reading in the world. *Understood Betsy* by Dorothy Canfield Fisher was the first book I checked out and took home to enjoy. That first book and others were read, sometimes more than once before I returned them. But each one just whetted my appetite for more.

There was no television, no radio, and nothing quite equaled the satisfaction of settling down with a book and making the acquaintance of a whole new cast of characters. Some were so good I couldn't keep them to myself, but insisted upon reading aloud to my mother, as she stood at the ironing board or bustled about the kitchen.

Sometime later, it was decided the library could do without a full time librarian, and Miss Batchelder accepted a position with the Stevens Memorial Library in Andover, Massachusetts, where she remained until she retired. She maintained an interest in the local library, however, and often stopped in on frequent visits to a friend, Miss Lena Reid, a teacher at Martinsburg High School.

On a visit to Martinsburg in 1964, she recalled there were 3,639 books in the library that first year, and these were kept moving by 2,800 regular borrowers. Records at the end of the year showed that 54,167 books were borrowed. This was in addition to the reference books used on the premises.

Noting that at the time of her visit the library was located in the City Hall building, she replied that it had "gone up in the world, and that's not necessarily good." She was referring to the fact that it was on the second floor and therefore inaccessible to those who for health reasons or physical disability had to avoid stairs. She felt at least as many adults as children should be using its facilities because they had little access to school libraries or other sources available to the youngsters. But that remained the library's location until the present one was built.

I recall my first visit to the present library when it was "brand-spanking new" as people used to say. Its elevators and gradually-sloped ramp eliminated any problems of inaccessibility and offered to everyone the opportunity to enter and avail themselves of its treats. Its shelves at that time held more than 20,000 books, and it was claimed to have a capacity of 60,000, and its 15,500 square feet of space was climate-controlled.

Photo courtesy Martinsburg Public Library

The Martinsburg-Berkeley County Public Library as it stands today, "a handsome addition to the Public Square." In addition to the main library, which celebrated its 75th anniversary in 2001, residents of Berkeley County now have the convenience of three branches.

I left the library and crossed the street and stood looking at the corner of the Public Square where for months past so much activity had been underway. The new library building of handmade pink brick shone bright in the morning sun, a handsome addition to the Square. Grass covered the lawn area, and artfully placed evergreens and clump birch waved at each side of the front entrance. We had come a long way since *Understood Betsy.*

> ***The Martinsburg –Berkeley County Public Library stands today as a symbol of the determination of the citizens who for the past 75 years have sought only the best for this community.***

So the Martinsburg–Berkeley County Public Library stands today as a symbol of the determination of the citizens who for the past 75 years have sought only the best for this community. The main library operates 72 hours per week, more than any other public library in the state of West Virginia. There are presently 147,500 books on its shelves; 2,500 audio tapes, (featuring music and books on tape,) 1,400 video cassettes, 100 CD-ROM titles, and 270 magazine and newspaper subscriptions to satisfy the reading needs of the 32,500 registered borrowers. Interlibrary loans total 4,000 annually, and reference transactions total 600 weekly.

The main library offers for public access 12 Internet computers, four word-processing computers and two CD-ROM work stations. Additionally, the library hosts art exhibits and other interesting displays which are changed each month. It has been a fine-free library for almost a year now, since National Library Week in 2000. This means the library does not charge late fees for overdue books. The staff just urges borrowers to return the books as promptly as possible to enable others to use them.

Miss Batchelder's heart would be glad to know there are also three branch libraries in Berkeley County, where adults as well as children find reading material available. These are Musselman–South Berkeley Community Library in Musselman High School; Naylor Memorial Library in Hedgesville, and North Berkeley Public Library on Nestle Quarry Road in Falling Waters.

A large staff of devoted employees serves the library and its branches. Peggy Batten retired at the end of January this year after serving 25 years as director. Betty Gunnoe, who has been there since 1966, is now acting director. Others on the main library staff and their dates of hire are:

Lois Brady, assistant director, 1971
Crissy Johnson, cataloguer, 1975
Therese Hess, literacy coordinator and director, 1980
David Porterfield, automation manager and assistant director, 1980
Margaret Demer, circulation librarian and Literacy Jottings author, 1983
Sharon Morris, children's librarian, 1984
Keith Hammersla, reference librarian and assistant director, 1984
Barbara Hilliard, children's circulation librarian, 1986
Honnor Dorsey, circulation and book discussion leader, 1987
Jane Levitan, public relations coordinator and young adult librarian, 1990
Jane Clipp, circulation librarian and periodicals librarian, 1992
Carolyn Leporini, interlibrary loan librarian, 1993

Hope Miller, who started in 1973, serves as librarian at Naylor Memorial and North Berkeley libraries, and Jacque Seldeen, who started working at the main library in 1992, took over as librarian at Musselman–South Berkeley Library this year.

War Memorial Park

A community success story

Adapted from ***The Journal***
September 3, 2000

Berkeley County War Memorial Park is one of this community's most successful ventures ever! That fact has never been more evident than during this summer season.

There isn't a day that it is not being enjoyed by citizens of every age, young mothers or dads with their little ones, families picnicking, young people with their sports, or adults resting in the shade or enjoying the pool or miniature golf.

Hundreds of local people and visitors head for the park to enjoy the Labor Day Early Bird Breakfast. One of its most successful fundraisers, the breakfast has become the place to be early in the morning of the first Monday in September. The inviting fragrance of steaks and ham on the grill draws a crowd every time.

The park has a long history of being able to call on community support; in fact it was maintained entirely by such support for its first 30 or more years of operation.

Shortly after the end of World War II, a group of community-minded citizens, headed by the late Paul Buxton (Buck) Martin, Nelson Clarke, the late Jack Clohan, Phillip T. Seibert, and a number of others of like interests, formed the Berkeley County War Memorial Park Association to plan a memorial for those in the county who had given their lives in service to their country.

Contributions came from active organizations such as the American Legion, Veterans of Foreign Wars, the Elks and Moose lodges, Lions Club, Kiwanis Club, Women's Club, and others. They were boosted by donations from individuals such as the late Garland (Buck) Dunn, who gave of his time and energy as well and served as president of the park board for 12 years. The example set by these men, who had gone solely on their enthusiasm and determination, was contagious, and soon the project was underway.

The former Rosemont Park, a 15-acre property on North Tennessee Avenue, was selected as the site because it was available. The park, which was opened as a commercial enterprise in 1921, had been a popular spot for some years. However, it went bankrupt in 1935. The site consisted mostly of fields and a deteriorated pavilion and swimming pool. The newly chartered Berkeley County War Memorial Park Association first obtained an option on the property, then purchased it at a cost of $15,000.

Following the purchase, with the aid of organizations and volunteers, workers began to fence the area, repair and enlarge the swimming pool, build roads, construct pavilions, picnic tables, and fireplaces, everything needed to make the park a good place for community enjoyment. Memorial trees were planted, each with an individually engraved bronze plaque at its base.

Photo courtesy Berkeley County Historical Society

The former Rosemont Park in the 1920s. The site consisted mostly of fields and a deteriorated pavilion and swimming pool.

Garden club members volunteered their time and talent to plant and maintain flowerbeds.

Giddy with success, the board decided to keep the park a non-profit community project, determining not to call upon any governmental body for funds at any time. Further, they decided to enlarge its memorial coverage to include not only those who gave their lives in World War II, but those of World War I and other conflicts in this century as well.

Events began, some as fundraisers, others non-profit, but each quickly took on a life of its own, finding a place in the traditional life of citizenry. Some have been the Memorial Day Service by the veterans' groups, the Labor Day Breakfast, the Independence Day celebration and fireworks, the June Jubilee, the Sunday Evening Vesper Service sponsored by the Ministerial Association, automobile shows, and performances by musical groups. There are many, many others, plus the use made of the park for special occasions, family reunions and school functions. There are many other people who have been prominent in the history of War Memorial Park, but it would be impossible to name them all or to include the names of all of those community citizens whose foresight, volunteer contributions, and labor have made it all possible.

A memorial monument was erected in the park and dedicated with an appropriate ceremony, sponsored by the VFW Post 896. Master of Ceremonies, Chaplain Howard L. Fulk, offered the invocation, and Captain Hjalmar E. Swanson, USNR, was a guest speaker. Members of American Legion Post 102 participated in the ceremony, and Park Board Chairman B. Franklin Miles, Jr., was chairman of the monument committee.

In 1987, the Berkeley County Parks and Recreation Board, which had been formed about a year before, took over daily operation of the park, under the able leadership of Director Steve Catlett and his staff. A number of improvements have resulted, including a new bathhouse, renovation of the pool, a miniature

Photo courtesy Kathy Weaver

War Memorial Park today is a thriving venture and a community success story. Above, participants assemble at the park for the start of the annual Memory Walk of the Alzheimer's Association of Martinsburg.

golf course, and additional restrooms and play equipment in that area.

The park has grown to be even more popular and attracts other groups, which sponsor more activities. Some fine musical aggregations including those of the United States Army, Marines and Air Force, have performed to the delight of large audiences. A number of memorial pavilions have been added through the years, including one each for the late Dr. Howard Fulk and the late Ernest McKee. A cover was placed over the stage, as a memorial for Captain Swanson, given by his wife, Claire.

The past few years, the park has been the starting and finishing point for the highly successful March of Dimes Walk America, Heart Walk, and the Alzheimer's Memory Walk.

So, get up early every Labor Day and head out to enjoy a hearty steak and country ham breakfast with your friends and neighbors and, at the same time, support the Berkeley County War Memorial Park. You'll be glad you did! It's here for your pleasure.

People to Remember

Thanks, Dad

Adapted from ***The Journal***
Father's Day, June 14, 1980

Someone said that many great men are famous, but most great men are not.

He was not a famous man. He was a humble man; he could not have brought himself to be anything else.

If you can recall the years before 1949 in Martinsburg, you no doubt saw him many times. You might have seen him on his way to work in the morning—but you would have to be up and out early, for he worked a long day at the mill.

You might have seen him on his way home in the evening, his gait a bit slower perhaps than in the morning, for he believed in an honest day's work for an honest day's pay. Nonetheless, he would have been swinging his lunch box and whistling low a favorite tune, his eyes alert behind the gold-framed glasses and his hand ready to wave a greeting.

Chances are, if you stopped to chat with him, he told you the history of the building across the street or the railroad in Martinsburg or an anecdote about your father that was new to you, for he stored up facts about people and places prominent in local history.

He hadn't much formal education. Perhaps at a very young age he didn't feel he wanted it or needed it. Or maybe he was bored. His father was a schoolteacher, so it would certainly seem that he could have had more schooling if he'd wanted it.

But he never stopped learning, and history was the subject nearest to his heart. He could not bear to see a good book discarded, especially history. It was to the despair of his wife that he would salvage such books and carry them home to add to the collection.

Once he procured such a book, it became his constant companion in his favorite chair in the corner behind the stove, until it was read from cover to cover and its facts added to those already in his well-stocked memory.

Study of the Civil War meant the most to him. His father had joined the Union Army and served in the Medical Corps, and he delighted in pointing out the Maryland School for the Deaf in Frederick, where his father was stationed during the war.

You might have seen him on a Saturday morning when he oiled the lawn mower, turned it upside down, put the hand clippers in his hip pocket, filled his pipe with tobacco and started on the trek to the cemetery.

Once there, he took great care in mowing and cleaning the cemetery lots and trimming by hand around the graves where his mother and eldest daughter were laid to rest within five days during the influenza epidemic of 1918. There were others of his family there as well, including a second daughter who died in infancy.

He used to tell of a bright summer day, many years before, when as a boy he had been playing in a nearby field and found a berry that made a bright red stain. He decided to play a great joke on his mother and covered himself with the stain, then went home crying, pretending he was injured.

He found the house in an uproar. Word had just been brought that his 19-year-old brother had been killed by a train while at work on the railroad. No one noticed the little boy covered with berry stain, and he went to the pump on the back porch and washed himself clean.

He was not a famous man, but he left a legacy of greatness, a legacy of love.

He knew much sorrow, but he never let it get him down. He was known for his sense of humor and his harmless pranks; he would never knowingly hurt any man. He would never have taken the Lord's name in vain. His sole vice was his pipe, and he laid it aside only when he had a handful of cigars—the epitome of luxury.

In his lodge he held the office of prelate for many years. Proud were the days when he wore the uniform in parades. He was well aware of the solemnity of the black and gold robes, but his heart was too light to be pinioned beneath them, so he nodded and winked to friends along the way.

He was walking up the little street he loved one bright fall day when he was felled by a stroke. He lived only five more days.

He was small of stature, but he stood tall. He stood for all the things he knew were right and condemned all the things he knew were wrong. He loved his God, his church, his family, his lodge and his fellow man.

He was not a famous man, but he left a legacy of greatness, a legacy of love.

Photo from author's collection

Ethel's parents, Anna and Wilbur Wayble, of whom she writes with admiration and fond memories.

My Mother's Garden

Adapted from ***The Journal***
May 9, 1999

It's almost Mother's Day, and it's impossible to think of my mother without thinking of her garden, for I believe it was her greatest joy.

When the spring rains had moistened the fertile ground and the sun was beginning to warm it a bit, her eyes glowed with anticipation. She went out to the shed and got her well-worn spade to dig into the rich loam and get ready to plant the seeds she had ready for her garden. She raked the soil smooth and carefully lined up the rows.

From that point on, she spent many happy hours doing whatever it took to bring her project to fruition. If the season was dry, she could have a problem because it cost extra money to use the sprinkler or garden hose. The water bill was one thing, but if you wanted to water your yard or garden, you had to have a hose license, and that cost $5.00 extra a year, and extra dollars weren't always available.

We had a water-powered washing machine. Ever hear of that? I have no idea how it worked, but you fastened the hose to the machine and turned on the faucet to operate the motor. She didn't see the point in wasting the fresh water from the washer by letting it run down the gutter after it passed through the washer motor, so she connected the lawn sprinkler to it on wash day.

Someone from the water department showed up one day and told her she was watering her flowers without a hose license. When she showed him how she was doing it, he allowed her to continue, and she was proud of that victory.

Somehow, her garden always turned out beautifully. She could be seen from early morning every day, weeding, transplanting, or doing whatever was necessary to care for her beloved plants. Her bonnet was a bright flower among the rows of beans, peas, squash, cabbage, radishes, onions, cucumbers, kale, beets, salsify, carrots, parsnips, corn, tomatoes, lettuce, Swiss chard, and others I've forgotten.

Then came the many hours spent gathering her harvest, sharing it with family and friends, and preserving a supply for the winter months. She canned, she pickled, she made sauces, jellies, and preserves, anything she could learn do with her bounty. This was well before anyone thought of freezing fruits and vegetables. A few people had pressure canners, but she had her long wash boiler and her gray enamel canner, her pride and joy.

The wash boiler fit on the cookstove in the kitchen and the canner was placed on the Oriole gas range in the corner. The jars of vegetables had to be boiled three or four hours, and with the two stoves going full-blast and the water boiling, the heat was intense in our little low-ceilinged kitchen.

But any discomfort was forgotten when she displayed with great pride the shelves filled with the fruit of her labors and invited friends and relatives for tasty meals or prepared a dish for a neighbor who was "feeling poorly."

Not all of the products of my mother's garden were edible, however. She took great pride in her flowers. She grew a variety of these, but she loved her roses best. My father shared her love for the roses, and in the summer we always made certain he had a fresh rosebud pinned to his lapel when we left for Sunday School and church

My mother was a very determined woman. I'm not sure she

> ***Along with her garden and flower seeds, my mother planted seeds of willpower and determination.***

was ever talked out of doing something she really wanted to do, and I don't remember ever hearing her say "I can't." She always said , "I don't want to hear you say you can't! You can do anything anybody else can do if you try hard enough. Somebody else might do it better, but you can do it if you try."

I've tried to live by that precept, and do you know what? I think she was right!

Along with her garden and flower seeds, my mother planted seeds of willpower and determination as well.

John W. Dean

Spanning 90 years of local history

Adapted from ***The Journal***
February 2, 1965

I guess you might say the most unusual thing about my life is that I was born, reared, and schooled and spent my entire life right here in Martinsburg, without ever having worked or attended school a single day outside of my hometown."

Thus begins the story of John Wesley Dean, 90 years old today, whose life has spanned the greatest years of progress in the history of mankind, from the covered wagon days of his grandparents to the age of space travel.

Mr. Dean's appearance belies his age by at least 20 years. There's an infectious twinkle in his eye, he carries himself well, and he wears his full head of hair in the "distinguished statesman" style.

He was born February 2, 1875, son of James William and Emily Virginia Snodeal Dean, who had been married at the home of Mr. and Mrs. Howard Boltz, 419 West King Street where Dunn and Seibert now stands. His father had come here from Orange Court House, Virginia, and his mother was a native of Berkeley County. His birthplace was the house still standing at 221 Winchester Avenue, in a block which figures prominently in the story of his early years. Just across the street at number 218, his grandfather, John W. Snodeal, had his home and grocery store.

At number 220, Mr. Dean's grandfather had a shop where

coaches, carriages and sleighs were made, and where covered wagons stopped for repairs enroute north and south. Conveniently located at numbers 212-214 was a blacksmith shop run by the family, and at the rear, his grandfather's livery stables, where he always kept six or eight gaited horses, under the capable care of several young boys.

> ***There's an infectious twinkle in his eye, he carries himself well, and he wears his full head of hair in the "distinguished statesman" style.***

The property at number 210 had been sold by Mr. Snodeal to a Mr. Houck, a miller, who walked daily to and from work at Kilmer's Mill on Dry Run Road. The old tollgate was situated in the one–story house at the corner of West John Street and Winchester Avenue, now Fultz' Confectionery.

When Mr. Dean was one year old, the family moved from the house on Winchester Avenue to 214 South Raleigh Street, renting a two story rough casted house from Mr. Buser, assistant postmaster. Later, the family built the home at 212 South Raleigh, where they lived for some years.

Young John's first schooling was in the Third Ward School, now John Street School, which was converted from a livery stable and was shared by a large storage room and a room used for practice by the City Band.

There were four rooms in the school, two grades in each, and the teachers he recalls include Miss Jenny Alburtis and Alonzo Ryneal. The latter's sister, Miss Molly Ryneal, later taught at Burke Street School. (Mr. Dean's mother attended this school, and later his children were also to get their first schooling there.)

At the age of 16, Mr. Dean lost his father, who died at the age of 40. There was no recourse but to drop out of school to give his mother a hand with the family. He had been attending the then "new" high school at the corner of Stephen and South Queen streets, where he was a junior.

He started work as an errand boy at Bender's Lumber Company, where the Union Sales Company is now located. The company made handcrafted mantels, stairways and other pieces.

The Rev. L. DeWitt Gerhardt, Sr., who was serving as the first principal of the high school, started operating a private school at his home, 419 West King Street, coincidentally the same house where Mr. Dean's parents were married.

Mr. Gerhardt sought out the boy, whom he had found to be a promising student, and persuaded him to attend evening classes in his private school. Here young Dean completed his education by attending from September to June for four years, receiving the equivalent of two years of college at that time.

Much in evidence is the beautiful Spencerian script learned during those years, still written and shaded by a firm hand.

With the additional education thus obtained, he moved up in the business at Bender's, becoming assistant bookkeeper and then bookkeeper for three years. This led to a position as bookkeeper for a Mr. Evans who ran a wholesale tobacco business on the corner opposite the B&O Freight Office. He later became salesman for Mr. Evans.

From that time until he went into business for himself in 1906, he worked at various times as salesman for Evans, Shaffer Grocery Company, and J. H. Miller and Son, wholesale grocers, all of whom were located at what is now Exchange Place, in the vicinity of the North Queen Street subway.

He married Miss Daisy May Schill in 1901 in St. John's Lutheran Church, where he still holds membership. The couple became the parents of five children: John W. Dean, Jr., Greenville, Pennsylvania; Miss Mary Dean, at home; George S. Dean, Park Avenue, and two children who died in childhood. Mrs. Dean died August 26, 1960.

Mr. Dean went into business for himself in 1906 at the corner of Martin and Queen Streets, now Diamond's, where he sold furnishing and merchandise. He later bought the building from the Blondell family, and in 1921 sold it to the Kirsons.

This was followed by a move to the Berkeley Hotel building, where he continued his men's tailoring business until 1939. He then went into the insurance business for the Farmers and Mechanics Mutual Fire Insurance Company in the Shenandoah Hotel building, staying with the company until his retirement in 1959.

In community activities Mr. Dean is still active in the Lebanon Chapter, Royal Arch Masons, where he served as recording secretary for 50 years, and as one the earliest members of the local Rotary Club, where he served as recording and corresponding secretary for 25 years.

One of his fondest recollections is the service he gave in promoting Chautauqua during the early 1920's. He also enjoyed promoting the formation of the first Business Men's Association.

Remarkable as is his story up to this point, it has a very refreshing turn in that the story of John Wesley Dean is not all looking backward. He still maintains a vital interest in all about him and in current events.

Although he confidently expects to reach age 100, he says he will need 30 or 35 more years to see all the things come to pass that he predicts, and he can't feel sure that he will be blessed with that many more years.

But who knows? With all the strides made in medicine and the excellent health and vitality he displays, we would hesitate to dismiss this possibility.

Editor's note: **John Wesley Dean died August 2, 1973, at the age of 98 years and six months to the day.**

Photo courtesy Bob and Ruth Ann Dean

A stately John Wesley Dean, dignified and impeccably dressed. In his early 90s when this photograph was taken, his appearance, said Ethel, belied his age by at least 20 years.

Velma Bergdoll Johnson

Adapted from ***The Journal***
February 14, 1971

Her goal sounded like a simple one 35 years ago—to teach home economics to women and girls—but in achieving it she has touched more homes in the community with her influence than perhaps any other person.

The ink was hardly dry on her B.S. degree in Home Economics when Miss Velma Bergdoll of Petersburg came to Berkeley County fresh from West Virginia University in June of 1935 for a meeting of the Berkeley County Home Demonstration Council and to accept the position of home demonstration agent.

J. O. Knapp, director of the Agricultural Extension Service of WVU, presented her to the group. She distinctly remembers the faces of Mrs. James E. McDonald, Mrs. C. M. Speck and Mrs. Fenton Gall; Mrs. Paul Lingamfelter was council president. The late Carroll Miller was on hand to cover events for *The Journal*.

The council had been formed September 24, 1920, with Mrs. H. L. Smith as president, and Mrs. Harlan Thatcher as secretary. Miss Gertrude Humphreys was state leader of home demonstration work, and there were nine clubs in Berkeley County, founded on the following dates: Swan Pond, 1918; Tuscarora, 1919; Pikeside, 1920; Vanclevesville, 1920; Berkeley, 1927; Spring Mills, 1927; Gerardstown, 1933; Bunker Hill, 1934, and Inwood, 1934. The Swan Pond and Berkeley clubs have since disbanded.

Almost immediately, she was caught up in tri-county 4-H camp. Others assisting in that camp were W. N. McClung, county agent, and Ernest VanMetre, 4-H agent, of Berkeley County; Neil Bolton, county agent, and Oliver Johnson, 4-H agent, of Jefferson County; and W. C. Willey, county agent, and Edna Cole Yost, home demonstration agent, of Morgan County.

Mr. VanMetre took her as a guest to her first meeting, that of the Gerardstown Club, at the home of Miss Emily Schoening.

Although she went right to work, young Miss Bergdoll must have had a bit of time for personal interests, for she won the heart of K. Brent Johnson, an underwriter for the New York Life Insurance Company and a native of Hedgesville. On February 3, 1940, they were married in Winchester, Virginia, and have lived in Martinsburg since that time. They built their home on Red Hill Road several years ago.

Mrs. Johnson taught primarily through the home demonstration and 4-H clubs, but she also has given programs for many women's organizations, PTA groups, youth organizations and other community efforts. She has led young women's conferences at Bardane, at Shepherd College, and in Martinsburg for Berkeley, Jefferson and Morgan Counties. In 1968–69, a newsletter for young women was published and sent out to a mailing list of about 2,000.

Under her leadership, clubs continued to form in the county. These included: Marlowe, 1938; Arden-Tabler, 1940; Bedington, 1940; Fairview, 1949; Opequon, 1950; BIG, 1958; Potomac, 1963 (now disbanded); Tomahawk, 1968, and Belle Boyd, 1969.

The goal of these clubs is a program of education through the university's extension service. The program brings out its own leaders through training, and they take back to the clubs lessons learned. Use is made of other sources of information, the agent herself, specialists from WVU, and competent persons from the community, as well as visitors from other countries.

Mrs. Johnson's voice became known to thousands, as she

began a radio schedule of five one-minute spots on WEPM in 1962, and included WCST in Berkeley Springs in 1967. At that time she began to work actively with the HD program in Morgan County and continued until her retirement January 1, 1970.

Velma Bergdoll Johnson at her desk at the WVU Extension Office before her retirement in 1971. Johnson had served for 35 years as Home Demonstration Agent for Berkeley County.

Photo from Journal article

Mrs. Johnson's professional affiliations include membership in Phi Upsilon Omicron (home economics honorary at WVU); Epsilon Sigma Phi (extension honorary); American Home Economics Association; and National Association of Extension Home Economists, from which she received the award for Distinguished Service in 1947. She served on the executive board of the National Association for eight years, two of which she was president.

An active member of the American Association of University Women, she has held a number of offices, including presidency of the Martinsburg Branch. She is a member of First Baptist Church, and teaches the Fidelis Sunday School Class.

Her professional improvement includes attendance at Arizona and Colorado State Universities. She is listed in *Who's Who of American Women*.

These are the professional qualifications of an individual who has worked with thousands of women in the Eastern Panhandle for 35 years. Her influence upon these women and girls is immeasurable and will continue to be reflected in their homes for generations.

Mrs. Johnson was honored at the annual Achievement Day at Trinity United Methodist Church and received a gift that expressed the appreciation of the club members. She was also honored at a retirement party hosted by the Berkeley County Agricultural Agencies. Plus, agents of the Keyser area honored her at the home of Franz Taylor in Keyser.

Since retiring, Mrs. Johnson plans to see more of her mother, Mrs. Ed Bergdoll, who lives on the family farm near Petersburg, and to have more time at home with her husband, who now has his offices at home.

In general, she expects to be less busy, but those who know her certainly wouldn't bet on it!

Master of His Craft

Legacy of local shoe repair shop ends

Adapted from ***The Journal***
August 1, 1981

While he was growing up in Martinsburg, young Joseph Leporini dreamed of becoming an "Ivy Leaguer," but fate intervened. He became a shoe repairman and a master of his craft.

When Leporini sold his business in the Public Square in Martinsburg to Levi Folk at the end of June, he entrusted to other hands the service given by him and his father for 74 years.

"In 1918, my father, Paul Leporini, purchased a shoe repairing shop from Mr. Pat Apicella," says Joseph Leporini. "The building, then known as the Hobbs Building, was later purchased by Dr. William Wallace and Dr. John L. Daniels, and is now the location of the Worldwide Travel Service.

"Because of remodeling, he later moved to the corner of King and College streets. The place had been occupied by the American Express until it moved to the B&O Station on East Martin Street."

Still seeking a better location, the shop moved to the Hotel Berkeley building in 1926, where it operated 43 years until 1970, when the old hotel was demolished to make way for the new Citizens National Bank.

The elder Mr. Leporini had died in 1957, and his son was operating the business himself. One more move in 1970 took the business to the Boyd Building in the Public Square, and this is its present location.

While attending grade school and high school at St. Joseph's, young Joe helped out in the shop after school, shining shoes or working on the finisher, using black or brown ink and wax.

"Boy! I hated that job!" he says. "You tell youngsters what happened during those Depression years, and they laugh. They imagine you're telling a story or a joke. But, this really changed my future, because of all kinds of misfortune.

"All my relatives lived in Philadelphia," he says. "My mother's brother said it was a must that when I graduated, I was going to live with him and his family so I could attend Pennsylvania University. The only expense would be tuition and books.

"But what happened? The same year that I finished school he died. So, because of his death and the Depression, which came on in full force, all the dreams vanished." The disappointment still shows in his face. "The only alternative was to master in shoe repairing, and I have done this until now.

"There are many recollections of those years in our shop. During the Depression we were all in bad shape financially. I remember people had to go barefooted until they got a written permit from Mrs. Maude Mason (of the County Department of Public Assistance) to repair shoes for them and their children so they could go to school and to work—if they had a job. Sometimes we had to wait over a month before we got paid, and this was a hardship for us."

(Leporini didn't mention it, but local citizens recall that many youngsters were able to go school because the Leporinis repaired their shoes at no charge when they were unable to pay.)

"I remember that during the Second World War, because of shoe rationing, people had to have their shoes repaired because they were allowed only one pair of new shoes a year per person. Our shop was swamped with shoes to be repaired. We used to pile them up on the floor, separating them for each day of the week.

Many days we were compelled to draw the curtain and lock the doors to keep people out so we could get some work done. We worked from 7 A.M. to 11 P.M. every day except Sunday. The Lord was good to us to survive that period with good health."

People brought in umbrellas, alarm clocks, baby carriages, and even denture plates to be glued or to have loose teeth replaced.

There were humorous times, too, although with a bit of pathos. Leporini says one would not believe the items that were brought into a shoe shop to be repaired. People brought in umbrellas, alarm clocks, baby carriages, and even denture plates to be glued or to have loose teeth replaced. Many went away disappointed, for there was nothing he could do for them.

Many people dropped into the shop for friendly chats, and there were some pretty good arguments with regard to sports. Leporini has always been an ardent sports fan, although he says his only active participation has been "to fight with shoes."

In 1930, Joseph Leporini and Irene Domenico, daughter of Mr. and Mrs. Camilla Domenico, were married in St. Joseph's Catholic Church, and on August 4, 1980, the couple celebrated their 50th wedding anniversary at a surprise reception arranged by their children.

"We have been blessed with three children," says Leporini, "now all grown up. Justin married Arelia Corradi from Rome, Italy, and Paul married Carolyn Scott from near Columbus, Ohio. Both sons are veterans of Vietnam. Justin retired from the Army as a sergeant first class and lives in Orlando, Florida. Paul is employed with Univac–Sperry Rand Computers in Parkersburg. Rosa, after some years of employment in clerical work in

Washington and Baltimore and in the lab at King's Daughters Hospital, had a nervous breakdown. She is at home with us and attends the Eastern Panhandle Training Center. We have six grandchildren."

Friends and customers have asked him why so few are taking up the shoe repair trade today.

The principal reason, he says, is the fact that although shoe repair is a skilled craft, it is not recognized as such, and for this reason he would not permit either of his sons to follow in his footsteps.

"You are regarded by some people as low," he says. "I have two sons, and I kept them out of the shop all the time, because I didn't want them to get involved in this life as it happened to me. The last two years in Baltimore alone, 90 shoe repair shops went out of business. The reason? They got jobs with other industries, in construction work and other kinds of labor, under union jobs. They work shorter hours for higher wages and get hospitalization and all kinds of benefits. Plus, during working hours they get coffee breaks and other kinds of breaks and vacations. You can't blame them. They work 40 hours, and after that get time-and-a-half. You don't get any of these benefits in this involvement.

"There are places in this town where people who work with a bucket and mop make $6 and $7 per hour, and time-and-a-half for overtime. Do we make this kind of money? Not a chance. They get paid vacations so they can enjoy themselves. If we go for a few days vacation it comes out of our pocket and the money we lose we feel for months."

A problem which has evolved during the last few years and is most discouraging is the reaction of people when they bring in shoes to be repaired and are told the cost.

"Materials are high and scarce, but when they are told the job will cost $17 or $18 to repair they hit the ceiling and say, 'I can go and buy a new pair for that!'"

"Now this is a very stupid statement," say Leporini. "This

make of shoes costs from $50 to $100 a pair. Now, who is the loser? But even worse is when they bring you work and don't come back to pick them up. Not only do you not get paid for your work, they rob you of your materials that you have bought and paid for. Some of your best friends will do this and show no remorse whatsoever! So you give these shoes to some charity organization, or else you may get mad and put them in the garbage."

Leporini says he never wanted to see his place closed, and never gave up hope of having someone take it over and continue the business. As he puts it, "I wanted to hand it over to someone to take care of people in the community, be a good craftsman and live with the reputation of the Leporinis for workmanship and service. So I was lucky in finding such a man in Levi Folk. He is not only expert in shoe rebuilding, but in orthopedic work and in making belts, handbags and other leather items.

"Believe me, this has been a very hard decision for me to make. I have had my social security card since 1973, when I was 65. But I would not retire, because I could not stay home. This work was in my blood and I could not live without it. But when I reached my 73rd birthday June 27, because of age and other sickness and affliction, I thought it was time to draw the line. In the words of a ball player, I had to hang up my glove."

He expresses appreciation to the many friends and customers who encouraged him to stay in business, letting him know they needed him, and to countless others who said they would pray for him.

"This really gave me a lift," he says with emotion, "and it really helped me to carry on. I hate to say goodbye, or, as we say in Italian, "arrive derci." I hope to spend the rest of my life here in the community I have always loved. Many friends have come to see me, saying they miss me in my place of business. I hate to admit it, but I couldn't help but break down with emotion—to know you have so many friends who love you—and I must say I love them the same.

"I wish all kinds of good fortune for many years to come to Levi Folk, who purchased the shop. I am happy to have found someone who can maintain Leporini's Shoe Service's integrity and give this community good service in this field. I want to express my appreciation to all the people we have served, especially all our long-time customers and their families. These people will never be forgotten."

Photo from Journal article

Joseph Leporini on the job before his retirement in 1981. Leporini's Shoe Service was a local shoe repair legacy and family-owned business for 74 years.

Folk, who came here from Hancock, West Virginia, brings 20 years experience in the shoe repair and leather business gained in the Georgetown, South Carolina, area. He plans to keep the name of the shop the same and to broaden his line to include a wide range of leather items, polishes, shoestrings, bags, luggage, and orthopedic supplies, and he will repair anything capable of repair.

"If the community will give me a chance, I will give the same good service the Leporinis have given through the years," he promises, adding, "and Mr. Leporini is welcome to come in here and putter around, or work, or talk with his friends any time he wants to!"

Seeing the smile break over Leporini's face, one is sure he'll do just that, for as he said, "This work is in my blood."

Some Who Served

Nurses Lift Spirits, Touch Lives

Adapted from ***The Journal***
June 1, 2003

The nursing profession has seen many changes since Dorothy (Dot) Evans Leavitt donned her crisp white cap and starched uniform as a member of the class of eight graduates of the King's Daughters Hospital School of Nursing back in 1940.

Over a cup of tea recently, she reminisced about those years in training. Martinsburg had two hospitals at that time, each with its own training school. The original City Hospital, which was founded by Dr. T. K. Oates, was located at the corner of West Burke Street and South Maple Avenue. King's Daughters Hospital, where Dot trained, had been converted from a jail many years earlier, and was in the old stone structure at the corner of East King and South Spring streets. The stone building adjacent to the hospital was the school of nursing.

Nurses in those hospitals were trained by the doctors and the several registered nurses who worked there. Dot recalls there were no registered nurses in charge of the floors. There was a nurse in the Operating Room and a laboratory technician. Mabel Fuller, R.N., was superintendent of nurses; Miss Laidley was supervisor of the Operating Room; and Miss O'Connell, R.N. and the physicians taught theory.

She remembers that Dr. N. B. Hendrix taught Embryology

and Dr. A. W. Armentrout taught Surgery. A partial list of early prominent local physicians includes Dr. George Martin, Dr. Victor Glover, Dr. Richard Talbott, Dr. Roger E. Clapham, Dr. Ernest H. Bitner, Dr. A. B. Eagle, Dr. C. G. Power, Dr. Halvard Wanger, Dr. Elizabeth McFetridge, Dr. Clifford Sperow, Dr. Marvin H. Porterfield, Dr. William Haltom, Dr. William A. Wallace (who had started as a pharmacist and later earned his medical degree), and, of course, Dr. T. K. Oates, City Hospital founder, and his son, Dr. Max O. Oates. Nelle Hess Wachtel, served as secretary and treasurer at King's Daughters Hospital for many years.

Photo from Journal article

Graduates of the 1940 King's Daughters School of Nursing. From left, front row, Phyllis Lewis, Doris Knicely; middle row, Elizabeth Hook, Genevieve Butts, Cora Welsh; back row, Lorine Groves, Dorothy Evans, Anne Peters.

The King's Daughters Hospital at that time had a few private rooms, some semi-private rooms, a men's ward and a women's ward. A children's ward was added later.

Other members of the class of 1940 were Phyllis Lewis, Doris Knicely, Elizabeth Hook, Genevieve Butts, Cora Welsh, Lorine Groves and Anne Peters. After graduation, each went her own way. Dot's first experience was in private nursing.

Shortly after, she went to work in the office of Dr. Wallace and had been there only five months when he went into military service. After his return, he became Martinsburg's first radiologist. Dr. Wallace began his practice in his home on South Maple Avenue and later moved to West King Street, just off the Public Square next to the Public Library.

At that location, he had a room set up as a laboratory, completely lined with lead to take X- rays. Dr. Wallace did fluoroscopy tests and read X-rays for the doctors and the hospitals. If a patient needed an X-ray, the doctor sent the person to Dr. Wallace's office. He took the X-ray; Dot mixed the developing solution, developed the film in the lab, and hung it to dry. Dr. Wallace read it and dictated his report into a Dictaphone. Dot typed the report and carried the X-ray and report back to the doctor's office. If an X-ray was taken at the hospital, Dr. Wallace went to the hospital and read it. Before that time, a doctor came over from Hagerstown to read the X-rays.

As an aside, Dot recalls that the typical doctor charged $1.50 for an office call and $3.00 for a visit to the patient's home. The doctor carried a black bag containing medicines, and there was an extra one dollar charge for these medications. She noted that after World War II, the cost of an office call went to $3.00. Dot worked for Dr. Wallace until her marriage in 1953.

Nurses played an important part in the Civil Defense program during the years following World War II, under sponsorship of the U.S. Department of Health, Education and Welfare. Since Dot had knowledge of the effects of radiation, she was asked to sit on the planning committee for the local community disaster plan. She has some well-worn books on the role of the nurse in community emergency health preparedness. "We were really prepared, at that time," she declared.

Still dear to her heart are memories of the volunteer hours she spent at the Newton D. Baker General Hospital, now the Veterans Administration Center. For 18 months during 1943–1944, she and other local nurses went nightly to the hospital after their regular shift, to help care for the wounded young men brought from overseas hospitals. Names of registered nurses she mentioned include Pauline Gregory, Julia Gregory, Kathryn Foreman and Lillian Voorhees, and there were others.

This experience led to the organization of the Newton D. Baker Paraplegics and Associates, a group made up of paraplegic patients, members of their families and volunteers, who came from a distance and met locally for dinner and fellowship for many years after the war. We remember, too, that this spirit of volunteering expanded into the community, and many other people gave hundreds of hours of volunteer work to the hospital during those years.

National Nurses' Week was observed in May with several local events. The first was a service honoring Florence Nightingale, who is credited with being the mother of nursing. This event was restarted 10 years ago by graduates of both local hospitals. Dot Simpson, R.N., and Ginny Reisenweber, R.N., supervisors at City Hospital, plan the annual service in which a graduate from one of the local schools of nursing is selected to represent Miss Nightingale. Katherine Snyder Smith, R.N., who is a 1946 graduate of City Hospital School of Nursing and worked there for over 30 years, was this year's Florence Nightingale. Sandra Cleaver, R.N., Chief Operating Officer of City Hospital, was the speaker. She was introduced by Nancy Gain Waikus, R.N., Director of Quality and Risk Management. Those attending were invited to share their memories and discuss the changes in nursing that they have witnessed through the years. This year's observance was held at the First Baptist Church on King Street. Refreshments and fellowship followed.

In the second observance, Christine White, R.N., a nurse in the Transitional Care Unit at City Hospital, received the coveted Ginny Jones Award. This award goes annually to the nurse who exemplifies nursing care at its best. It is presented in honor of Virginia "Ginny" Jones, who was a nurse at City Hospital for 25 years and was generally recognized as outstanding in her devotion and caring attitude toward her patients.

I was privileged to have Ginny as a neighbor many of those years, and found her to have the same caring attitude toward her neighbors. The busy mother of six sons and two daughters, she always maintained the same quiet, unruffled manner. I always marveled at that, and certainly can understand why she would be worthy of such recognition. My only regret is that we weren't able to spend more time together, because she worked nights and I worked days.

There have been many changes since the graduation of Dorothy Leavitt and her classmates, Katherine Smith and Ginny Jones. The field of nursing has expanded to include a diversity of opportunities, but today's nurse can still be inspired by the motto chosen for the 2003 observance of National Nurses' Week: *Nurses: Lifting Spirits—Touching Lives.*

Martinsburg City Hospital

A hospital is more than blocks and stone and plastered walls. It's made up of the passion and compassion, the joy and pain of those who have lived, loved, laughed and wept within its halls, those whose skilled hands have brought forth life, repaired broken and pain-wracked bodies and, when their skills were not enough, or the bodies were too old or too tired, have given aid and comfort to those left behind.

Adapted from ***The Journal***
February 20, 2000

The above paragraph opened a story I wrote February. 21, 1974, at the time of the razing of the Old City Hospital, which was being replaced by the fine, modern hospital now on Tavern Road. Let's take a look at the beginning of City Hospital, quoting freely from several histories written by the late Dr. H. G. Tonkin, Judge Gray Silver and others involved in the hospital

It's impossible to tell the story of City Hospital without first sharing the story of its founder, Dr. Theodore Kensell Oates, for it is impossible to separate the two. The hospital is the result of the vision, dedication, and unceasing effort of a young, intelligent and caring young man who devoted his life to bringing about its existence.

One cannot help but marvel at the result of his work and realize the pride he would feel in the hospital we have in Martinsburg today. But let's start at the beginning.

In 1904, Dr. Oates, a young man of 35, closed his practice in Capon Bridge and came to Martinsburg. At the time of his arrival, there was no organized hospital such as exists today. He was a pioneer in the field of surgery, about which little was known and which many doctors were reluctant to accept. At that time, about the only surgery performed was amputation of an arm or leg following an accident or injury. These were done under the most primitive of conditions at the scene of an accident or any available place, and were performed mainly by Dr. Newton D. Baker or Dr. S. N. Myers, who were employed by the B&O Railroad.

Martinsburg was a railroad town with shops where car repairs were made, and injuries were frequent. Just as surgery was almost unknown, anesthesia was unheard of, and the victim could suffer untold misery at the hands of those who were attempting to save his life.

There were no operating rooms and no schools of nursing. After several public meetings failed to result in creating either operating facilities or a school of nursing so that the practicing surgeons would not be forced to operate in private homes, Dr. Oates purchased a residence at the corner of West Burke Street and South Maple Avenue.

Here he opened his facility with an operating room and beds for three patients. This soon became so overcrowded that three years later he started, single-handedly, a limited hospital, looking to facilities for adequate hospitalization and the training of nurses. He employed the services of W. H. Whitson, a local architect, to draw plans and specifications for what at the time must have seemed a rather imposing structure.

It was a 12-room, three-story hospital, built of concrete blocks manufactured locally and raised to their position by horsepower. This served as a main part of the hospital for several years. A fourth story was added in 1909 and a four-story brick addition in

Photo courtesy Berkeley County Historical Society

Martinsburg's first City Hospital as it stood in the early 1900s at the corner of West Burke Street and South Maple Avenue. Founded by Dr. Theodore Oates, the early structure consisted of 12 rooms and three stories. The fourth story shown above was added in 1909.

1926. This expansion brought it to an 85-bed hospital.

A school of nursing had been started at the hospital in 1906 with Martha Silver, a graduate of Johns Hopkins University School of Nursing, as its first superintendent. The continual growth of the nursing school to meet ever-expanding needs made it necessary to provide quarters for the nurses. A property on West Burke Street was purchased and a nurse's home was built there in 1910.

Interesting stories abound concerning the early hospital. The first abdominal operation to be performed in this section of the state was by Dr. Oates in 1905. Since facilities were not complete, it was necessary to perform the operation upon a kitchen table in the patient's home. Instruments were sterilized by boiling them in kitchen utensils on the stove. The patient had acute appendicitis with perforation and peritonitis. Thanks to the skill of the young surgeon despite adverse conditions, the patient had an excellent post-operative convalescence.

Shortly afterward but also before the hospital unit was completed, Dr. Oates performed another operation upon a young man suffering from a hernia. This, too, was performed in a home, but by this time, Dr. Oates had purchased an operating table and it was moved to the home for the work. Dr. G. B. Hedges administered the ether.

The first craniotomy (brain surgery) in this section was performed by Dr. Oates upon a young man who had suffered a head injury. His recovery also proved satisfactory.

Dr. H. G. Tonkin, one of the hospital's early supporters, recalled that due to the limited surgical facilities, most ill patients had felt they were going to the hospital to die. But, with the coming of Dr. Oates and his hospital, this was all changed, and people felt they had access to a good surgeon and a good hospital. It was no longer necessary for doctors to send their patients needing surgery to Baltimore, a trip many were denied because of physical condition or the delay or expense involved.

Dr. Oates himself was the 42nd patient in City Hospital, when he submitted to an appendectomy December 25, 1907, performed by a former classmate, Dr. Bruin of Strasburg, Virginia.

In his history, Dr. Tonkin recalled some personal facts in the lives of these medical pioneers. To quote:

"While some doctors were located as far away as Hancock, most had to travel to see their patients by horse and buggy, and it was the rule rather than the exception to see patients in the home, rather than the hospital. It was about this time that automobiles were coming into use, and a few of the doctors purchased them. Dr. Oates was among the first to buy a car, and he bought a red Reo roadster, of which he was quite proud. It was shortly after this that I purchased my first car.

"It was quite a sight in the early days to see and hear them running about, it being necessary to carry extra tires and tubes, tire irons, pumps, jacks, pliers, patching equipment, penknives, for the frequent punctures, as well as wrenches, spare parts, spark plugs and many other items. These, together with instruments and bags, all contributed to the general clatter."

Through the years, many prominent, interested citizens have supported the hospital through its board of directors, the school of nursing and its volunteer program. The late J. Franklin Larkin, long-time local grocer, was the first child born in the hospital, and the late Mrs.Hannis Porter, the former Alberta Arnica, was the nursing school's first graduate.

In 1939, Dr. Oates presented his interest and persuaded the other stockholders to present their interest to a board of directors to form a non-profit corporation to own and operate the hospital. In essence, this meant that the hospital was an outright gift, as the deed specified that it be perpetuated, owned and operated by the residents of this community.

In 1936, Dr. Max Oates, the only child of Dr. T. K. and Altha Oglesbee Oates, returned to Martinsburg to become associated with his father in the practice of surgery, bringing with him new ideas and modern techniques.

He had come to Martinsburg with his parents in 1904 and attended local schools. Following graduation from Martinsburg High School, he entered Johns Hopkins University, where he received his degree in 1925 and graduated from the School of Medicine in 1929. He served as an intern in the Department of Surgery at Hopkins, then went to Durham, North Carolina, in the summer of 1930 for the opening of the Duke University Hospital, where he remained for six years, completing a residency and serving as an instructor in pathology and surgery. He remained here to serve as superintendent of the City Hospital following the death of his father in 1951.

Many community citizens have been supportive of the City Hospital through the years and helped the dream of its founder become a reality. As can be readily understood, there were a number of ups and downs financially.

Dr. T. K. Oates underwrote most of the cost until 1909, when the sum of $25,000 in stock was sold upon incorporation of the facility. When the brick addition was added in 1929, it was necessary to raise more than $35,000, a large sum in those Depression days. This was accomplished by the personal endorsement of Oates and a prominent local businessman, W. R. Caskey.

However, troubles continued to plague the young hospital. Debts to banks climbed to $40,000, and additional indebtedness amounted to $30,000. Also advanced to Oates were notes in the amount of $30,000, which he took from the corporations.

In 1939, a new corporation was formed with perpetual existence, and the stockholders of City Hospital, Inc., conveyed the hospital property to the board of trustees. Oates and his son, Dr. Max O. Oates, along with Clarence W. Martin, Jr., Dr. W. E. Minghini, and Gray Silver, Jr., were incorporators. Clarence E. Martin, Sr., served as attorney.

The indebtedness was gradually liquidated, with the exception of the notes held by Oates. Thus it was that in 1948, he canceled these, plus the interest, and turned them over to the board of trustees to make the hospital debt-free.

During this period and for some years following, it is recalled that one out of five patients was unable to pay for needed care, and this amounted to a loss of some $32,000 annually, again, a large sum for that time.

In 1955, the board of trustees and staff celebrated the hospital's 50th anniversary with a program dedicated to its founder, who had died February 4, 1951. Dr. Max O. Oates, was superintendent and treasurer at that time. Other officers and trustees were: U. G. Potts; R. L. Tay, secretary and assistant treasurer; Dr. Curtis G. Power; U. Robert Fierro; R. C. Williams, president; Dr. H. G. Tonkin; Louis Cohen; Dr. George O. Martin; Gray Silver Jr., vice-president; Paul H. Bowers; James M. VanMetre; Luther H.

Caskey; Harvey Beeler; and Clarence E. Martin, Jr.

The Rt. Rev. Harry Lee Doll, D.D., suffragan bishop of the Episcopal Diocese of Maryland and a Martinsburg native, was guest speaker for the occasion.

By the late 1950s it became evident that Martinsburg needed a larger, more modern hospital, and the board of directors began looking for a site. Interested citizens began a fund drive and hospital volunteers added their work toward that end. Let's take a quick look at these volunteers.

Through the years, hospital volunteers have come in several forms. First was the hospital auxiliary, organized in 1916 by 26 women of the community. It had grown by the following year to 60 members. The group met three or four times a year, depending upon the need, and the members paid five cents a month dues. The women made fancy work, held exchanges (now known as bring-and-buy sales), had dollar campaigns and birthday banks, and contacted the Farm Women's Clubs and the schools to aid in collecting money.

Each fall they spent days peeling apples and boiling apple butter in iron kettles over an open fire in the lot behind the hospital. This was sold to buy china, glassware, food, and furniture, and to host parties for the nurses and student nurses, as well as to purchase hospital equipment.

In 1940, the auxiliary made 52 gallons of apple butter, sponsored a bingo party and sold magazine subscriptions.

When the first class of students was ready to graduate in 1921, the auxiliary purchased invitations for the graduates and served refreshments. At this time the Junior Auxiliary was organized for those people who could not attend daytime meetings and to give student nurses a chance to help with hospital expenses.

During the 1960s and 1970s the sewing committee mended more than 1,000 pieces monthly and found time to make new items for the hospital and patients, such as covers for food trays and bedpans, rag dolls, sheets, and pillowcases.

In 1976, one of the members was honored for having given 2,600 hours of volunteer service. In 1986, a 70th anniversary celebration was held at the annual dues tea. Despite bitter cold weather, 71 women gathered to pay dues and welcomed six new members. The Junior and Senior auxiliaries had consolidated at that time and boasted a membership of 131 members, each paying dues of $2 a year. At that meeting, the hospital administration expressed appreciation to the auxiliary for its purchase of a televised patient education system, which was to bring vital education into each patient's room.

During the 1980s and 1990s the women purchased microwaves for each floor, television sets, a birthing bed, furniture for the waiting room, rocking chairs, wheelchairs, a medical alert system and new clothing for newborns.

In 1983 the auxiliary participated for the first time in activities of the West Virginia Hospital Association, and representatives began attending the annual meetings at The Greenbrier in White Sulphur Springs. It has had state winners for Auxiliary of the Year and two district winners for Auxiliary of the Year.

City Hospital, born of one young doctor's dream, moved into its present location on Dry Run Road in 1972.

Today, volunteers can be seen throughout the hospital, their jackets and badges adding color and their bright smiles and willing hands offering aid wherever needed.

The present City Hospital sits on a 37-acre site on Dry Run Road, purchased by the board of directors at a cost of $74,000. That same year, the West Virginia Board of Health in Charleston approved a grant of $532,369 for construction of a new hospital.

This was only the beginning, of course; the goal was to have a 135-bed hospital ready to open in 1970.

That goal was made possible by a grant of $1,750,000 from the federal Hill-Burton Act; a grant of $319,421 from the Appalachian Regional Commission; and a 40-year loan of $1,500,000 with an interest rate of 4.25 percent from the Economic Development Administration of the U.S. Department of Commerce. The board of trustees was responsible for raising the remaining $719,123, with $614,000 already in cash assets. The remaining $105,000 was expected to be raised locally through contributions during the construction period.

A contract was formally awarded to W. Harley Miller, Inc., local builder, January 22, 1969, following approval from the West Virginia State Health Department and the U.S. Public Health Service. The contract was for $3,473,408, and the groundbreaking was tentatively planned for early February. Cost of the entire project was estimated at $4,288,544. This estimate included $815,136 for cost of equipment, architect's fee, site survey, soil investigation, and land purchase.

The City Hospital, born of one young doctor's dream, moved into its present location on Dry Run Road in 1972. In 1977, it merged with the King's Daughters Hospital, which had been founded by a non-sectarian group and transferred to the Sisters of the Holy Ghost in 1951. The merger was to avoid duplication of services and provide the best possible health service to the community. It was preceded by local controversy because people of the community were divided in their loyalty to their favorite hospital. But it resulted in a modern health care environment with a highly trained and dedicated staff and the most up-to-date hospital equipment, which today's citizens view with pride and confidence.

Ground-breaking ceremonies were conducted in November of 1979 for a $17 million project to dramatically expand the first floor and add four additional floors to the hospital. The addition gave the hospital 135 more in-patient beds, bringing the total to 260 beds, and with space for at least 27 more when needed. New, sophisticated, state-of-the-art equipment was also added to keep pace with medical advances. Two new elevators were added, as well as extensive safety and security systems to provide a safe environment.

Hospital Corporation of America, which had considered building a hospital in Martinsburg, made an offer of some $8 million for the hospital, which was rejected. At that point, HCA, the largest hospital management corporation in America, sought and obtained a contract to manage the local hospital for the following 20 years. In the late 1980s, the management, then known as Quorum, recommended a re-structuring under the Gateway Regional Health system. This now includes two Panhandle nursing homes, Carehaven on the Charles Town Road, and Canterbury in Shepherdstown.

The Dorothy A. McCormack Cancer and Rehabilitation Center is the latest addition to City Hospital. The ribbon-cutting

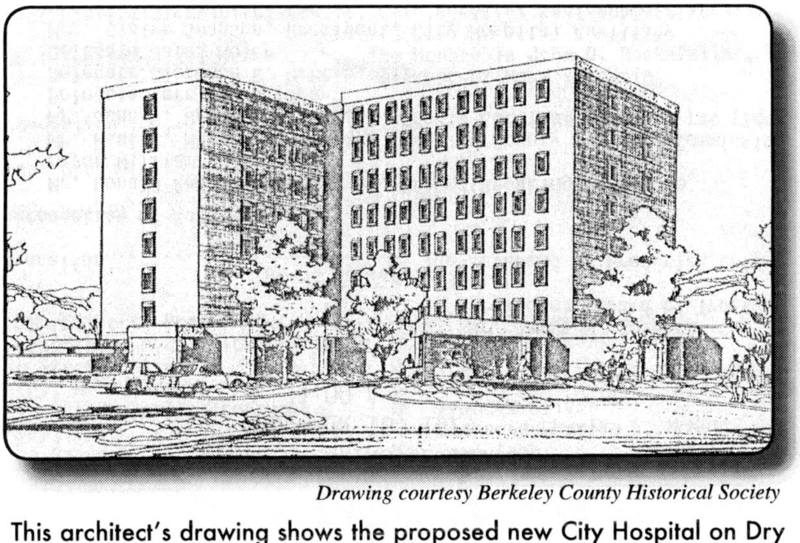

Drawing courtesy Berkeley County Historical Society

This architect's drawing shows the proposed new City Hospital on Dry Run Road at the time of its ground-breaking ceremony in November 1979.

ceremony was held on a bright Saturday afternoon, September 18, 1999, before an enthusiastic crowd.

Leonard J. McCormack, who donated $750,000 toward the center in memory of his wife, Dorothy, was the principal speaker. He retold the story of how he and his wife began receiving their health care at City Hospital. Fighting cancer, Mrs. McCormack had been a patient there more than once. After her death in 1998, her husband, looking for a permanent memorial to her, was told of plans for the center. His decision to support the project was two-fold. First, he felt it was the perfect way to honor his wife's memory. Secondly, he wanted to give something back to the community and felt there was no better way than to make sure cancer patients would not have to travel out of state to receive their radiation therapy.

The three-story brick facility not only houses cancer radiation therapy, but includes expanded physical therapy and rehabilitation services, Business Health Services, The Wellness Center (a hospital-based fitness center), behavioral health, American Cancer Society Resource Center, and physician office suites.

In short, at the moment the ribbon was cut, the Gateway Regional Health Foundation's dream of "bringing great strides in healthcare closer to home," became a reality.

Since the opening of Tri-State Radiation Oncology, occupying part of the first floor of the Dorothy A. McCormack Cancer Treatment and Rehabilitation Center, patients no longer have to travel out of town for their treatments.

The need for this therapy became apparent when studies revealed that in the Eastern Panhandle 300 new cases of cancer were predicted annually, and it was also estimated that 25 to 30 percent of these patients would need radiation therapy in fighting their cancer.

In many instances, cancer radiation therapy is required five times a week over a course of several weeks. Having to make so many round trips out of town and back is hard on patients and families, both physically and financially. The opening of such a unit locally keeps patients within the community, in an environment they are used to and where they are most comfortable—a significant addition for the Eastern Panhandle.

In his column, *Looking to the Future,* Jon D. Applebaum, who succeeded Peter J. Mulford as Chief Executive Officer, says, "As we close the decade of the nineties, it is important all of us reflect on our past achievements. As the new millennium approaches, it is equally important to look forward to our future potential.

"The dedicated professionals of City Hospital and the Gateway Regional Health System will continue to assess the medical needs of our community to ensure that the best possible care is available to our residents. Newer, more effective diagnostic tools and treatment protocols will be developed in efforts to continually improve our healthcare delivery system, thus opening new doors. In the future, an increasing emphasis will be placed on health promotion and preventive medicine to improve the overall health status of our community.

"As City Hospital enters its second century of service to our community, we are committed to continuing our mission to serve as a recognized leader in the provision of high quality, cost-effective healthcare and wellness services for the residents of the Eastern Panhandle."

Re-elected as members of the Board of Directors for the 2000 term were: Dr. Frank A. Hamilton, Jr., chairman; J. Wayne Lancaster, vice chairman; James H. Rickard, secretary; and Douglas M. Widmyer, treasurer.

Retaining their positions as members at large are Donald T. Anderson; Dr. James Brown; Dr. Jeffrey DeBord; Betty Gunnoe; Dr. D. Ewell Hendricks; Dr. James B. Hutzler; Max O. Oates, Jr.; Scott Roach; Gray Silver, Jr.; and the Rev. Patrick Walker.

Evelyn S. Oates, who retired from the board in 1993, serves as assistant treasurer and member of the finance committee. Her husband, Dr. Max O. Oates, who was named superintendent of

Photo courtesy City Hospital

Martinsburg City Hospital has come a long way since its humble origin as a 12-room downtown structure. The hospital will celebrate its 100th anniversary in 2005.

the hospital in 1941 and served as chief executive officer from 1951 until his retirement in 1976, continued as treasurer and board member until his death on February 9, 1983. The Board of Trustees is ultimately responsible for the future direction and operations of the hospital. Board members donate their time and expertise.

Members of the Medical Staff Committee are Dr. James E. Brown, president; Dr. Timothy K. Bowers; Dr. Jeffrey B. DeBord; Dr. D. Ewell Hendricks; Dr. Jesse Jalazo; Dr. Terrence Reidy; Dr. Jack F. Shamblin; and Dr. Robert S. Strauch.

Senior Managers are Jon D. Applebaum, chief executive officer; Sandra Cleaver, assistant administrator; Gary W. Broadwater, chief financial officer; Kathleen E. Wotring, chief nursing officer; Larry Stratmann, human resources director; and Dr. George Chapman, director of Medical Staff Affairs.

No attempt has been made in this story to name all of the citizens who have played a part in the growth of the hospital through the years since its founding by Dr. Theodore Kensell Oates, a dedicated, highly intelligent, visionary small-town doctor. But they are legion. We can be proud of each one of them and of the fine City Hospital now serving this community.

King's Daughters Hospital

A look at its beginnings

Adapted from ***The Journal***
November 7, 1999

The history of King's Daughters Hospital, now a vacant stone structure at the corner of East King and Spring streets, is well-known to longtime citizens, but may be unfamiliar to some of our new residents. Besides, it's an inspirational story and fun to read.

The King's Daughters was the name of a group of local ladies who were organized May 3, 1890, with the stated purpose "to work among the poor and needy in His Name," wherever they saw the need. Little is known about their early work because their first minute book was lost. But one incident resulted in the founding of the King's Daughters Hospital in a building constructed about 1798, originally for use as a jail.

In the early 1890s, Martinsburg was a railroad center, with shops for repairing the locomotives, and accidents were frequent. When a man was injured, he was placed on a stretcher and taken to an empty room in the railroad station or to the jail—the only places available. Then one day a mother gave birth while traveling on a B&O passenger train en route from the west. She and the baby were taken from the train on a stretcher by Dr. James Whann McSherry, the railroad physician, and sent to the jail.

"Dr. Jim" (as he was affectionately known throughout the county) called his sister, one of the members of King's Daughters, and said, "Pat, you've always wanted a hospital. Get your girls together. I've sent a patient to the jail." She eagerly called them together, and they went to the jail, made mother and baby comfortable, and cared for them until they were ready to travel, with the little one outfitted in clothing sewn by the group.

A bit later, the old jail was put up for sale. The King's Daughters purchased it January 9, 1893, at a cost of $2,610, and it was paid in full March 15, 1894. The group elected a board of directors October 24, 1895, and adopted a constitution and bylaws for conducting the business of the hospital circle of the King's Daughters.

Although they are long departed, names of this first board of directors are remembered in the history of the hospital: Miss M.G. (Pat) McSherry, Mrs. George Roush, Mrs. George P. Blessing, Mrs. Daniel Mattaei, Mrs. J. W. Pitzer, Miss Louise Westfall, Mrs. M. G. Tabler, Mrs. W. N. Lynch, and Mrs. Nannie Henshaw. Miss McSherry was elected president, Miss Lulu Muth, secretary, and Mrs. Blessing was treasurer.

At that meeting, the board of directors voted to accept the offer of a loan of $2,600 from Dr. McSherry for improvements to convert the jail into a hospital. Even before improvements were completed, patients began arriving and were cared for by the Hospital Circle of King's Daughters.

There are many interesting and heart-warming stories of the untiring efforts of this group of women. One patient, a tailor named Charles L. Foster, who, according to the minutes, had "a lame limb that bothered him for some time," stayed at the hospital for an extended period. When he died, he left his entire estate to the King's Daughters. This was their first legacy. It amounted to $50 and two bolts of cloth. The ladies cut carriage robes from the wool, bound them with silk braid and sold them to raise funds. But their benefactor was not forgotten. They then got busy soliciting donations and started a fund to place a stone at his grave.

Photo courtesy Berkeley County Historical Society

King's Daughters Hospital, now a vacant structure at the corner of East King and Spring streets, was purchased in 1893 and opened by a group of local ladies whose mission was "to work among the poor and needy in His Name." The building was originally constructed in the late 1700s for use as a jail.

The second patient was a Mr. Swartz. Miss Kate Stewart and her brother were given living quarters in the building and were hired to care for him at $5 a month. The rent from Mr. Swartz's house helped defray expenses. At that time, the women carried food from their own homes to feed the patients.

The circle soon found it necessary to start fund-raising in the community. They had entertainments, suppers, and did all kinds of community work, but all of their own services were free of charge. When the remodeled jail was opened May 15, 1896, it was dedicated "to the Glory of God" and offered to the doctors for the use of their patients, "irrespective of race, creed, or politics." A two-day reception followed. Suppers were sold at 25 cents a plate and the circle netted $135 for their two days of work.

The stories of fund-raising by this group of dedicated women are endless, particularly during those early years. Community support was outstanding. Money was donated, equipment contributed, rooms were furnished, gifts of all kinds and voluntary service were given to the hospital and the hard-working women who ran it. Churches made contributions, children gave entertainments at their schools to raise money, and patients and other individuals gave contributions of up to $5,000, a considerable sum in those days.

One incident revealed in a history recorded by Mrs. G. J. E. Sponseller almost didn't work out. A firemen's convention was held here May 5, 1904, and the circle was asked to serve a dinner for 200 delegates. As was their custom, they worked hard and prepared a hearty dinner for that number—to have only two firemen come to dinner.

The dinner was to be served in Fellers Hall at the corner of Race and Queen streets, the only community hall in the city at that time, where all dinners and dances were staged. Several of the women went uptown to see where the firemen were and found the trouble. They discovered the dinner was too far from where the action was taking place.

Undaunted, they called a friend, George Roush, to bring his horse and wagon to the hall, and they put the food into tubs and other containers and loaded it onto the wagon. The parade of women marched behind the wagon to the best location close to the jolly crowd. In no time at all, the food was sold and more had to be prepared.

In 1913, The King's Daughters reorganized and became the King's Daughters Hospital Circle. They were given a charter by the state and authorized to conduct a Training School for Nurses, issue diplomas, and confer degrees. The school opened September 14, 1914, with a class of 15 young women. The Superintendent of Nurses was Mrs. Florence Knapp of Providence Hospital, Washington, D.C.

Miss Margaret Beard entered training January 3, 1915, filling a vacancy of one student who resigned. Students were allowed $8 per month and room and board for three years. Later, the student monthly allowance was amended to $8 for the first year, $10 for the second and $12 for the third.

The uniform adopted had a high "bishop's" collar and long sleeves with crisp white cuffs, and the hem of the skirt had to touch the top of their high-top black shoes. They wore black hose and white caps. Upon entering, students were on probation for three months. Later, that period was extended to six months, after which the student received a cap.

Classes were held from 8 A.M. to 9 P.M., with the doctors and superintendent of nurses giving lectures in anatomy, general medicine, bacteriology, obstetrics, pediatrics, gynecology, surgery, laboratory, drugs and solutions, nursing techniques, and history of nursing.

In 1914, the same year the training school was opened, the hospital was remodeled and a fourth floor added. The operating room was moved to the fourth floor, and three sunrooms, a large porch on each floor, an elevator and a new kitchen and heating plant were installed.

In 1916, a rumor circulated that the school had no charter and graduates wouldn't be allowed to take State Board exams. All the students left except for Miss Beard, who was in her second year at the time. It was necessary for her to affiliate with the University of Maryland at four-month intervals for pediatrics, obstetrics and dietetics, which she did in 1917.

Miss Beard, therefore, became the hospital's first nursing graduate in 1918. The first commencement ceremony was conducted at the YMCA on West King Street. Dr. E. C. Stewart of Winchester delivered the address, and Mrs. George Roush presented the pin, a Maltese Cross encircled by a wreath. Miss Beard held the position of Metropolitan Life Insurance visiting nurse for many years. Later, she returned to work in the Obstetrics Department of the hospital until her retirement.

Community support of the hospital was evidenced by many dramatic incidents. During the influenza epidemic of 1918, the hospital was over-crowded and most of the nursing staff fell victim to the disease. Members of the Circle worked in the office, the kitchen, and as nurses or aides during the day, and the Catholic Sisters of Charity also volunteered their services, assuming night duty under the direction of Sister Madeline.

King's Daughters was one of only a few hospitals in the country that was organized, owned and managed by women for the use of doctors of the community and the care of their patients.

One of the things the nursing staff was proudest of was the Crippled Children's Section, which received great assistance from the Elks, the Junior Civic League and other public-spirited groups and individuals. The Hospital was unique in one important respect. It was one of only a few hospitals in the country that was organized, owned, and managed by women for the use of doctors of the community and the care of their patients.

According to a history of the hospital, the vision of two women and the loyal support of the public made it all possible. The first was Miss Pat McSherry, who, in the beginning, saw the need and encouraged a band of women to purchase the old jail. After Miss McSherry's death, Mrs. H. P. Thorn spearheaded efforts of the King's Daughters Circle to purchase the McSherry Home, the Crippled Children's Home, the Rodgers Home and other properties, and finally begin construction of a new King's Daughters Hospital about 1944.

General community fund-raising efforts, however, were not enough to keep pace with ever-rising construction costs, and after much discussion, the King's Daughters Circle voted to seek outside help. Finally, the Catholic Charities group of the Diocese of Richmond was contacted and the matter was referred to the Sisters of the Holy Ghost, headquartered in Pittsburgh. As a result, the entire project was turned over to the sisters to complete the building and operate a community hospital. This was accomplished and work resumed on the hospital in 1953.

After completion of the new facility, the old hospital became the King's Daughters School of Nursing with dormitories for students and classrooms for instruction. Student uniforms were changed to plain white with a KDH School of Nursing emblem on the sleeve. The graduate cap, designed by Virginia Robinson Walper in 1921, remained the same.

Over the years, students affiliated to the University of Maryland for Pediatrics, and Sheppard-Pratt Mental Institution for Psychiatry. Later they turned to the Philadelphia General Hospital for this training, and to Shepherd College for some of their classes.

But the class of 1973 was the last to graduate from the King's Daughters Hospital. In all, the school had turned out 444 nurses, an impressive record.

The new hospital served the community for 23 years until, plagued again with financial difficulties and with understandable reluctance from staff and nurses, it merged with City Hospital in 1977. That merger produced one of the finest hospitals in the eastern United States.

Camille Brown O'Rourke, R.N., closed her historical address at a reunion of the King's Daughters Alumnae with the following comment:

"Our K. D. Hospital may be gone, but every K. D. nurse can be proud she was a graduate of the King's Daughters Hospital School of Nursing. Our hospital and our school will live in us and through us as we work among the sick and needy 'In His Name.'"

The hospital has become the King's Daughters Court, a home for our older citizens. A plaque now hangs in the lobby bearing the names of nurses who graduated from King's Daughters Hospital School of Nursing. Many are working in hospitals in the area or in private duty nursing. Thus, Camille's prediction has proven true.

Caring for the Departed

A look back through the years

Adapted from ***The Journal***
July 29, 2001

Take a good look at her, Honey," said the lady who carried me on her arm, "because you'll never see her again." I was three years and three months old, and we were looking at a pretty girl in a white coffin in the front room of our house. She wore a pink dress and white stockings, and her hair lay in brown ringlets about her shoulders.

This is the only clear memory I have of my sister Frances. She was 13 years and 10 months old when she died during the influenza outbreak of 1918. The woman who held me was Viola Shipper, one of the neighbors who busied themselves about the house, bringing and preparing food and comforting my parents. Several friends came and sat in the dining room, drinking coffee or cocoa and talking all night for several nights, as was the custom. The "wake" was a very important part of mourning.

I remember little of this, but know that on the third day, the pastor of the United Brethren Church, Rev. W. F. Gruver, came to the house and conducted the funeral service. Then everyone followed the ornate, horse-drawn hearse to Green Hill Cemetery, and Frances was laid to rest beside her sister Nellie May, who had died of pneumonia 10 years before, on her second birthday.

This was typical of the handling of the deceased in those days. Funeral parlors were in existence at that time, but most folks were

Photo from author's collection

Three-year-old Ethel, front, and her 13-year-old sister Frances in 1918. Frances died shortly after this photo was taken during the influenza epidemic. The funeral service was conducted in the family home as was customary in those days.

"buried from the home," as it was expressed. A "crape," (a graceful sort of sash) was hung on the front door, marking it as a home in mourning. Thinking back on that time, I started wondering about this area's early funeral homes or funeral parlors. My research showed there have been more of them than I realized. Just how many and their dates of origin are not always easy to determine.

The city's first funeral home on record was started in 1842 as the Wilen Funeral Home. Its first location was on North Queen Street, over the former Moose Club. Adolph Kogelschatz, Sr., joined the firm in 1862. Some years later his nephew, Adolph Fayman Kogelschatz, bought out the business and with Robert G. Coffman, Sr., as his partner, opened the Kogelschatz & Coffman Funeral Home. They built on West Martin Street at the corner of College Street. This was sold many years later to the Jewish Congregation for use as a synagogue.

After Adolph's death in 1950, his son Louis W., III, took over the business. A graduate of Augusta Military Academy and Duke University, he had served as an infantry captain with the "Panther" Division in Europe. He took his professional training at Renaurd School for Morticians in New York.

He purchased the former Roush home, West King Street and Rosemont Avenue, and moved the funeral home to that location. This was one of the homes on the former Roush farm, and was

UNDERTAKERS

Kogelschatz & Coffman

UNDERTAKERS AND EMBALMERS

Oldest and Most Reliable House in the City

203 N. Queen Phones: C. & P. 41-W, C. V. 260 Wilen Bldg.

built before the Civil War. Robert G. Coffman, Sr., had also passed away and his son Robert, Jr., went into the business for a short time.

Still later, Alva Linder bought Coffman's share, and the firm became Kogelschatz & Linder Funeral Home. This was the situation when Louis, III, an active churchman and community leader, died at the age of 58, in 1974. His wife, Phyllis Kidwell Kogelschatz, provided the information for this account.

For several years, his sons, Louis W., IV, and Adolph Frederick, operated the funeral home, but they were not interested in continuing the business, and in 1984 it was sold to Charles M. Brown, who, with his father, the late Howard K. Brown, were operating the Brown Funeral Home. The Brown Funeral Home also has an interesting history.

An interview with Charles Brown, who currently operates the business, reveals that his grandfather, Charles Mortimer Brown, came to Hedgesville from Frederick County, Virginia, near Gainesville. He was a carpenter by trade. An ardent Republican, he served as postmaster in Hedgesville during the McKinley and Theodore Roosevelt administrations. One of the several men who served as mail carriers during that time was the father of the late K. Brent Johnson, a prominent insurance agent in Martinsburg.

In those days, coffins were wooden boxes built by skilled carpenters or cabinetmakers. It was a natural step for a skilled cabinetmaker to decide to become an undertaker and manufacture his own coffins. Charles says he was always told that his grandfather was a familiar sight as a professional, wearing a black plastic bow tie. His training consisted of weekend classes in Baltimore. He opened his undertaking business on Mary Street in Hedgesville in 1885.

He was one of two undertakers in Hedgesville at the time, one to lay away the Democrats and one for the Republicans. Brown's wife was the former Margaret Kyner, a native of Orrstown, Franklin County, Pennsylvania. Her father, Alfred

Kyner, had moved here and farmed on Sulphur Springs Road in Berkeley County, says Charles.

Howard Kyner Brown, Charles's father, was born in Hedgesville and attended Hedgesville High School. After leaving school he did odd jobs until he was drafted into the military during World War I. However, a heart flutter cut short his military career and he returned home and worked with his dad in the undertaking business.

He married Margaret Susan Seibert, daughter of Charles J. Seibert, on June 7, 1922. He trained at Eckles' Embalming School in Pittsburgh. The Browns moved to Martinsburg, present site of the business, in the spring of 1924, and it was here that Charles Mortimer Brown was born in 1926.

Howard Brown purchased the building from the Seibert estate in 1939 as a family residence. However, as conducting services in the funeral home became more popular, the family moved to South Raleigh Street and remodeled the King Street residence as a funeral parlor in 1941. It has since been remodeled twice, with several additions, in 1951 and 1961.

The historic building, constructed about 1852, was widely known in the 1870s as the Berkeley Female Seminary, operated by Miss Betty Butler.

Howard worked on the railroad in the 1920s, conducting his funeral director business only part time until 1930. His brother, Robert R. Brown, was associated with the business from 1930 until 1960.

Charles started working in the business officially after his discharge from the Navy in June 1947. During three years as a student at West Virginia University, he had worked for his dad during the summer months. In 1952, he went to embalming school, and noted that in January he will mark 50 years in the business.

In 1982 the company bought a former church in Ranson and opened the Jefferson Funeral Chapel. The stone chapel was built

Photo from Journal article

The Brown Funeral Home on West King Street was founded by Howard Brown in 1941. Howard's son Charles joined the business in 1952 and marked his 50th anniversary in the business in 2002.

in 1922 as an Episcopal mission and later became a Lutheran church.

In September 1984, the Brown Funeral Home Corporation purchased the Kogelschatz Funeral Home and operated that business as the Rosemont Funeral Home until a fire damaged the historic structure. In June of 2000, they built and opened the South Berkeley Chapel in Inwood. "Berkeley County has been good to us." Charles says.

Present stockholders in the corporation are Mr. and Mrs. Robert R. Rigot, Robert C. Fields, and Mr. and Mrs. Charles M. Brown. Employees whose faces have been familiar during the years at Browns include Jack Noll, Charles (Dude) Spring, Burney Branham, Johnny Arvin, Amelia Cole Hedges, Mary Ellen Lightner, Janetta Cross, Anna Mae Miller and others.

Other funeral homes that operated for varying amounts of time include Mose Cole Funeral Home on West Stephen Street; Charles P. Elliott Funeral Home on East Burke Street in the 1930s; Samuel Kesecker at Providence in Back Creek Valley; Weist's, in Gerardstown; and Hartzler's, Wimer's, and Rowland's in Martinsburg. Rosedale Cemetery Company has also had a funeral home and chapel on its grounds for some years.

The work of the funeral director today has greatly expanded since the days of those early craftsmen who first sought to care for the dead. It truly has become a service or a mission. Today's professional sees the family as a whole and employs a competent staff to work with the living, helping them with planning and counseling and comforting them in their time of sorrow.

Business and Industry

Auburn Wagon Works

A part of Martinsburg's early history

Adapted from ***The Journal***
February 27, 1974

Newcomers to this community may be a bit startled to hear the sound of a steamboat whistle daily at 6:45 and 7 A.M. and again at 5 P.M. if they realize that the only body of water flowing through Martinsburg is Tuscarora Creek.

That sound has been a part of the town since before the turn of the century, although not at its present location, National Fruit Product Company. It is one of the earliest sounds I recall from my childhood.

The whistle was first used to herald the start of the work-day at the Auburn Wagon Works on West Race Street, where Martinsburg Veneer Plant now stands, and remained there until the company closed down.

Max Robinson, first president of the company, came here from Auburn, New York. He resided on East King Street, at the present site of King's Daughters Hospital.

Frank J. Zill, also of Auburn, was foreman of the wheelwright department and lived on North Raleigh Street until building a home on East Burke Street. A Mr. Snoddy, first superintendent of the company, lived in the Fellers row on North Raleigh Street.

Farm wagons, the main product of the company, were sold locally through The Vehicle Company, which was located on West Race Street a few doors east of Raleigh, where a man by the

Photo from author's collection

Workers at the Auburn Wagon Works in the early 1900s. Ethel recalls her dad telling about the influenza epidemic of 1918, when the company switched temporarily from making wagons to constructing rough wooden boxes to accommodate the rising death toll. Ethel's father, Wilbur Wayble, is pictured in the back row, second from left.

name of Crim, from Bedington, was manager. Elmer E. Snyder was salesman and manager in later years, and at one time Daniel W. Shaffer, better known as "Cap," was also associated with the business.

Mr. William Schneider, who provided much of the information included here, recalls that about 1909, when the automobile had begun to replace horsedrawn vehicles, the Auburn Company sent a load of its wagons to Brazil, in the hope of building up a trade with that country. This, however, failed to materialize.

The wagon works was reportedly the first place in town to use a time clock system, according to Mr. Schneider. It was not an immediate success by any means, as it was deeply resented by several employees who were unhappy until they could be convinced that the system assured them full pay for time worked, thus protecting them as well as the company.

Mr. Schneider also recalls that the whistle was blown daily at 5:45 A.M. to give early risers the weather report in code. Where this information came from in those pre-radio days is questioned. It could have been provided by the *Hagerstown Almanac*—or perhaps the night watchman's corns!

I recall hearing my Dad tell about returning to work after the influenza epidemic of 1918 when our family had all been ill and my Dad had lost his mother and his eldest daughter within five days, and finding his co-workers busy making rough boxes. He became ill and had to come back home.

It wasn't too long after this that the company closed down. The buildings which housed it gradually deteriorated, and although several attempts were made through the years to start another industry there, the veneer plant was the first to succeed. Part of the building also houses several offices.

But the Auburn Wagon Works played an important part in the early history of Martinsburg.

Booth's Cycle Center

A family success story

*Adapted from **The Journal***
November 21, 1978

Booth's Cycle Center has been purchased by Mearle Spickler, and this brings to light a story about one of the city's oldest business houses.

Founder of the business, one of America's oldest motorcycle dealerships, was Harry W. Booth. Born in Paw Paw in 1877, young Harry came to Martinsburg, where his first job was as a baker for Rufus Caskey at Caskey's Bakery on East Race Street. Later he became chief baker for P. Otto Schneider at his bakery on West Martin Street.

The proud owner of an Indian Scout, he became interested in motorcycle repair. By 1912, the sideline had begun to pay his expenses, and he found he was able to bank his salary from Schneider's Bakery.

A wooden, four-car garage at 202 Winchester Avenue, owned by Wade Jones, became available, and he rented this building and went into business full time. In 1928, a neighbor, Vincent Grove, built the present concrete block building at the same location.

Mr. Booth continued motorcycle repair until Indian Motorcycle Company went out of business about 1957. After that, he concentrated on bicycles until 1962, when he obtained the dealership for the Honda motorcycle.

Two years later his health failed and he was hospitalized,

A young Harry W. Booth, founder of Booth's Cycle Center, on his 1912 Indian Scout. Motorcycles were always a part of his life, and repairing them proved to be profitable.

Photo from Journal article

thus the shop closed. Not wishing to see the business come to an end, he asked his son, Harry L. Booth, to come home and reopen the shop.

Although motorcycles were always a part of his life, the younger Harry didn't work in the business all the time. He had worked in a local grocery store for a while, and later, as a student of electrical engineering, was associated with the Pennsylvania Glass Sand Company of Mapleton Depot in the electrical division for two years.

He always loved to travel on his cycle and has a fine collection of postcards sent home from various trips, mostly to the western part of the United States.

In 1940 he took a civil service test for a job as a motorcycle mechanic instructor for the Army. First appointed as an inspector in the Quartermaster Corps at Camp Holabird, Baltimore, he was later assigned as an instructor at the Army Ordnance School, Springfield College, Massachusetts.

"From 1940 to '45, I was with the Army," he says. "After

'45 I went down to Bethlehem Steel and got on as an instrument technician—the instrument that controlled the furnaces—the engines—the earth actually trembles!

"But I was the only child, and Dad—well, he wasn't 'the old man.' He was my Dad, and he was in the hospital four or five weeks. He wanted me to come home and open the shop. I came home and opened the shop—and I've been here ever since.

"Then before he died in 1965, Dad gave me the business, lock, stock, and barrel, just gave it to me—and that was it," concludes Harry L. Booth.

He and his wife June, who handled the title and tax work,

Photo from Journal article

Harry L. Booth, center, son of Booth's Cycle Center founder Harry W. Booth, is shown with Mearle Spickler, left and Doug Spickler, right. The Spicklers purchased the business in 1977 after it had been in the Booth family for 65 years.

continued to sell Honda motorcycles until her death in 1972, when he sold that dealership and continued with bicycles.

He sold the shop in September 1977, but stayed around until after Christmas to help out the new owners, Mearle Spickler, president; his son Doug, vice-president and general manager; and Mearle's wife, Betty, described by her husband as the board of directors.

The Spicklers have no immediate plans for changes, the name will remain the same as it has for 65 years, and the same business policy will be in effect.

"Harry will be our consultant," says Spickler.

And with all those years of experience, he should know what he's talking about.

Matthews Foundry

The story of Berkeley's oldest business

Adapted from ***The Journal***
June 13, 1999

You may have noticed that a large stone building is now visible on the west side of North Queen Street just south of the railroad underpass. Its stonework was revealed in all its magnificence when Vincent Groh of Hagerstown purchased the former Matthews Foundry and razed the structures in front of it with a view to preserving the area for development.

We're eager to learn his plans and hope they're compatible with those of the visionary groups who want to develop a pleasant park and trail in the area. I know this would be possible, for I remember during my childhood in the late 1920s and early 1930s that we used to go to what we knew as "the falls" to go swimming (in my case, wading). This was a part of the Tuscarora Creek, somewhere north of the foundry along the railroad tracks in the vicinity of the National Fruit Products plant. That plant is also now owned by Groh.

The new owner has replaced the roof on the foundry building, but what other improvements he has made or is considering making will be interesting to learn. In the meantime, I'll tell you the history of the Matthews Foundry, quoting from a story I researched and wrote at least 25 years ago. Many of today's citizens were not living in Martinsburg at that time and may find it interesting.

The Matthews Foundry had a long and interesting history as Berkeley County's oldest continuing business. Fine ironwork was turned out at that location for 167 years, the last 100 of which the operation was under the ownership of the same family and was known as T. E. Matthews and Brother.

It's impossible to separate the history of the foundry from that of Martinsburg and Berkeley County because, as a matter of fact, it was older even than the state of West Virginia. To establish the setting, let's go back a few years. Berkeley County was a part of Frederick County, Virginia, until May 19, 1772, when it was established and named by Norbourne Berkeley, Baron Boutetort, Colonial Governor of Virginia under King George III.

Martinsburg had been laid out by General Adam Stephen, first high sheriff of the county, and established on 130 acres of Stephen's land in 1778 by enactment of the Virginia Legislature. The population was only a few hundred people, possibly as many as 1200.

A steady stream of packhorses and wagons brought pioneers through the town, as Martinsburg was situated on along one of several routes to the West. A number of former taverns have been preserved on farms in this area, and local historians have placed markers to keep alive the history of the county. In the early 1900s, there were some 50 gristmills on streams in Berkeley County, a like number of saw mills, and one paper mill.

In 1832, Samuel Fitz came to Martinsburg from Hanover County, Pennsylvania, and thought this a likely place for a foundry. Parts were packed across the mountains by mule train, and he established his foundry beside Tuscarora Creek, which flowed through the town. His original building is the one still standing.

According to an article in *The Martinsburg World,* an early newspaper, dated August 31, 1892, the foundry was established at a cost of $15,000, a handsome sum in those days.

The original building is described as stone, 140 feet long and

45 feet wide, containing two stories, each 12 feet high. The upper floor was used as a carpenter shop, 30 feet by 50 feet, a storage room 30 feet by 25 feet and an office, 30 feet by 30 feet.

In connection with his plant, Fitz operated two steam saw mills with a capacity of 5,000 feet each, one on the Cacapon River in Morgan County and the other on Back Creek near the village of Shanghai in Berkeley County. These two mills employed a total of 25 men.

The foundry was originally operated by water power, a dam on Tuscarora Creek operating two water wheels, one for a flour mill next door, also owned by Fitz, and the other for the foundry.

In those early days, the foundry was kept busy making parts for the wagons coming through, helping provide implements for the farmers, shoeing horses, and providing such needs for the community.

Then the Chesapeake & Ohio Canal was completed as far west as Williamsport, Maryland, in 1836, and this opened up faster routes to eastern markets than the Conestoga wagons and brought in supplies as well. Livestock was driven to the canal instead of over the mountains for many miles, and much merchandise was shipped by canal.

Then talk began of the B&O bringing a railroad through Martinsburg. In 1835, the railroad sent its surveyors in to lay out a route, and Martinsburg was on its way to becoming a boom town. The first steam engine passed through town from Harpers Ferry to Cumberland, Maryland, in 1842. A few years later a turnpike was laid between Winchester, some 22 miles south, and Williamsport, about 15 miles north of town. Martinsburg became the terminal of the turnpike in 1854 and about 1856 became the terminal of the Cumberland Valley Railroad.

Through these changing times, the local foundry, known at various times as the Tuscarora Repair Works and Tuscarora Foundry and Machine Works, was turning out castings, machine work for local industries, car wheels, cellar doors and steel plates used over downtown gutters to keep milady's long skirts out of the mud. It made repairs to engines, boilers, reapers, sowers, drills, threshing machines and sawmills and was the agent for the famed Tuscarora Plow.

The specialty of the founders, however, was the I-X-L Overshoot Water Wheel, which is known as the finest gravity wheel ever built. Perhaps the most famous still in existence is the 40-foot-diameter by 2-foot-face water wheel that drove the 35-barrel flour mill at Shepherdstown, 10 miles east of Martinsburg in Jefferson County.

Known as the Shepherd Mill, this mill was once owned by Shepherdstown Mayor Silas Starry and later by Ira Glackens. Described as the world's largest water wheel, it has been featured in National Geographic. Another of the foundry's famed water wheels is the Bunker Hill Mill, about 10 miles south of Martinsburg and believed to be in use still.

Situated as it was at the entrance to the Shenandoah Valley and on the main routes by both rail and turnpike, Berkeley

T. E. MATTHEWS J. D. MATTHEWS

T. E. MATTHEWS & BRO.

Foundry and Machine Works

All Kinds of Castings Made to Order
Work Neatly Done at Moderate Cost

C. & P. PHONE 75 W C. V. PHONE 137 W

MARTINSBURG, W. VA.

Manufacturers and Designers of the Martinsburg Electric and Gas "WHITE WAY POST," Iron Cellar Doors, Coal Hole and Cistern Rings, Snow Board Eagles and Irons. Valves of all kinds, Pipe and Pipe Fittings and Boiler Tubes. Contractors for Structural Steel I Beams, Channels and Angles, I Beams and Railing for Bridges. We have installed an Oxy-Acetylene Outfit for welding cast iron and all kinds of light welding.

County suffered greatly during the Civil War and was a battleground for troops. In fact, it changed hands a number of times, sometimes several times in a single day.

Every church or public building was used at one time or another as a hospital, barracks, stable for troops or either Union or Rebel soldiers.The community was divided in its sympathies. During this time, General Stonewall Jackson's men raided the foundry plant and took most of its machinery to Winchester, where he was headquartered.

Following the war, these parts were recovered. Martinsburg moved into recovery and developed as an industrial town, and the foundry was busy making parts for the mills, the quarries and other industries. Originally powered by water, it was later powered by steam, then gas, and finally, by electricity.

The original stone building bears another significant mark of history. There's a water line about 10 feet above the floor level

Photo courtesy Berkeley County Historical Society

Matthews Foundry, visible off North Queen Street along Tuscarora Creek, had a long and interesting history as one of Berkeley County's oldest continuing businesses.

that marks the level of Tuscarora Creek when it rose during the historic Johnstown, Pennsylvania, flood.

In 1894, brothers Thomas E. and Josiah D. Matthews, expert machinists who had worked for the company for some years and had erected its water wheels all over the country, bought out the business. Thomas, known as Uncle Ed, died about 1934 and Josiah took over operation of the foundry, assisted by his four sons, Charles A., Frederick J., Hunter A., and George E., the latter known as Eddie.

A fifth son, Theodore (Ted), was teaching school in Grafton at the time, but came home to teach in Berkeley County two years later and handled the bookkeeping.

After the death of Josiah in 1941, his sons continued the business. Charles died in 1959, Hunter in 1960, and Edward in 1967. Their mother had died in 1948. Brothers Fred and Ted continued the operation until Fred's death in 1985.

Fred's daughter, Lucille, and her husband, James Kearney, then took over the business and operated it until Kearney's death in 1997.

Some of the decorative wrought iron made there remains on a few Martinsburg buildings. The posts that held the "white way" lights on downtown streets, with their five large round white globes on each standard, of which early progressive citizens were so proud, were made by Matthews Foundry. These were removed some years ago, and no doubt the groups who are now trying to restore the downtown to its former appearance would give a fortune for them today.

Thus, the work of Berkeley County's oldest continuing business went on for 167 years, run by three generations of the same family for 103 years, a record indeed hard to surpass. The original building, now standing, is certainly deserving of its rightful place in the history of Martinsburg.

Mrs. Kearney recently sold the property to Groh, who has replaced the roof and razed the other buildings. This provides an excellent view of the old foundry from North Queen Street. Now let's hope proposed plans for cleaning up that area and making a park along Tuscarora Creek are supported and carried out. Then we'll have another historic spot to enjoy.

Interwoven Mills

*Adapted from **The Journal***
February 22, 1999

A recent news item mentioned the possibility of a dining room being opened in a portion of the former Interwoven Mills building and noted briefly in passing that men's socks were once manufactured there.

Believing this mill, which played an important part in local history and supported hundreds of families for decades, deserved more than a casual mention, I was prompted to search for notes I wrote some years ago while talking with the late William C. Schneider, whose remarkable memory was a valuable source of information for those attempting to compile local history.

Schneider recalled that when he was a boy he worked with Howard Staples, a water carrier for the builders, and later was hired in the boarding department of the mill. W. F. Mulliss was superintendent of the finishing department at that time, and Joseph Haas was the first foreman of the knitting department.

In operation during those early years was the Middlesex Plant, also known as the Kilbourne Mill. It was located on North Maple Avenue, and later became the Martinsburg Paper Box Factory. This plant was named for Middlesex County, New Jersey, which was apparently the home of the company's founders. John Mettler was one of the principal stockholders, as was Charles Kilbourne, and Frank W. VanHorn was plant superintendent.

Photo courtesy Berkeley County Historical Society

The Interwoven Mills, known as the Kilbourne Knitting Mills at the time of this 1917 photo, played an important part in Martinsburg's history, supporting hundreds of families for decades. The West King Street portion of the plant shown above now houses Panhandle Pottery and Design.

These two factories were known familiarly as the "upper mill" and the "lower mill."

The older mill was largely a knitting factory and had loopers until these machines were moved to the new location. Many families were supported by loopers, which sometimes were placed in private homes, where the woman of the house could work during those hours convenient to her. The work was hauled to the home daily, and finished work picked up by company trucks. One truck driver I personally remember was Joseph Fizer, who worked there for many years.

In 1908, the company began a big improvement project, digging out under the knitting department. Schneider remembered seeing dirt hauled by horse-drawn carts and used to fill up a dumping area, which is now Porter Avenue.

From that point west, during those years, all was open ground, strictly rural, with the two Roush family farms on either side of Tuscarora Road, now West King Street. The Roush homes still stand, one later becoming the Rosemont Funeral Home and now attorneys' offices, and the other once the Shimp home and now, I believe, an apartment building.

About that time, John Street was opened westward, Porter Avenue came into being, and King Street was extended. Schneider placed this about 1910–11.

At the top of the hill, where Tennessee Avenue now joins King Street, was a tollgate owned by the Berkeley and Hampshire Turnpike Company. (In later years, the Tollgate Confectionery occupied this location.) However, too many travelers avoided the tollgate by going out around, so another was added near the present home of Mr. and Mrs. Galtjo Geertsema on West King Street at Alabama Avenue. As might be expected, people resented these tollgates, for although they were ostensibly operated for the purpose of road maintenance, the roads were in very bad condition, and it was quite common for wagons or buggies to sink in the mud up to or over the hubcaps, Schneider said.

The Interwoven Stocking Company was a large, handsome, and prosperous plant, and was recognized and advertised as the largest men's hosiery factory in the world.

Meanwhile, the Interwoven continued to grow and expand operations. New sections were constructed on Porter Avenue and John Street. The ground floor was then used as a box factory and the finishing department was moved into most of the new section.

The portion of the plant on West King Street that now sits on a beautifully landscaped lawn and is used in part by Panhandle

Pottery and Design was at the time hidden from view by a row of houses and a grocery store. The store was at one time operated by Bill Kearns. The homes were occupied by families named Carper, Sonners, and Shipper, according to Schneider. The Shipper home was moved to South Rosemont Avenue and was later the home of the late Dr. Victor L. Glover. The others were razed.

The Interwoven Stocking Company was a large, handsome and prosperous plant, and was recognized and advertised as the largest men's hosiery factory in the world. Its whistle could be heard all over Martinsburg and was an integral part of daily life. Its first call of the day came at 6:45 A.M. to remind people to be on their way to work. (Almost everybody walked to work, of course, for many years). At 7 A.M. its sound indicated they should be on the job. At 12 noon, the sidewalks were filled as they left their jobs from the mills to head home or downtown for lunch. At 12:45 P.M. came the "quarter of" whistle reminding them to step it up and head back, where they worked until the 5 P.M. whistle dismissed them for the day.

Each New Year was welcomed in by long blasts from the whistle, joined by the foghorn sound of the steamboat whistle from Auburn Wagon Works and the whistles of steam engines on the tracks in the B&O Railroad yards. Later, the steamboat whistle was taken to the National Fruit Company plant in North Martinsburg. I've often wondered what happened to it when that plant closed.

According to Schneider, the Porter Avenue, Kentucky Avenue, and surrounding areas attracted builders, and a residential section came into being, largely as a result of the employees of the Interwoven, as had the southern section of town known as the "Boom," that grew up to be settled by employees of the Dunn and Berkeley Woolen Mills.

National Fruit Product Company

Personal memories spark a little nostalgia

Adapted from ***The Journal***
Fall of 1999

Seeing the former National Fruit Product Company building no longer in use, I remembered a morning 35 years ago.

While National Fruit was in operation, it was about this time each year that more than 200 community women began working hard, scrubbing and polishing windows and floors, washing draperies and slipcovers to make their houses shine in preparation for a few months of neglect.

A morning in early September brought these activities and the mounting suspense to a climax, and I watched the white-uniformed women gather early at the plant. The long-awaited summons had gone out and they were reporting to work, 100 women each shift for starters.

But as I mingled with them in line, it was almost inconceivable that the women considered themselves reporting to work. Sparkling eyes and friendly, cheery greetings were the order of the day, and it was easy to see they considered this more than work. It was a reunion—a coming-together of friends, many of whom had not seen each other since the fall before, and who were there to fellowship together while they processed the crop for the coming year. There was a unique closeness among them and it was obvious they thought of themselves as family.

A discussion with Margaret Dean and Dorothy Zombro, day and night shift supervisors respectively, and longtime employees,

Drawing courtesy Berkeley County Historical Society

Before Prohibition, the site of the former National Fruit Product Company in Martinsburg was a bustling Hannisville Distillery as indicated by the drawing above.

revealed that Plant Manager Paul L. Ayres deserved the credit for maintaining this family atmosphere. The much-admired Ayres was completing 29 years with the company that year, having come to the local plant from Waynesboro, Virginia, about 15 years earlier.

The company itself marked its 50th anniversary the year before my story. Before becoming National Fruit, however, the plant operated for several decades as Hannisville Distillery until being forced out of business by the onset of Prohibition.

The local division of National Fruit, in operation since 1919, was one of seven, the others being in Winchester, Strasburg and Timberville, Virginia; Atlanta, Georgia; Glassboro, New Jersey; and Kent City, Michigan. They employed a total of some 2,300 people during the processing season and produced scores of products under the "White House" label. Company headquarters were in Winchester, headed by Frank Armstrong, founder.

The Martinsburg plant employed about 550 on two shifts at full production, women outnumbering men four to one.

Surprises awaited the women the morning I was with them and they eagerly surveyed their surroundings. Facilities had been remodeled and modernized during the off-season and a welcome lunchroom had been added where hot foods were available. A new operation, sliced apples, was beginning during the new season. The usual local products were vinegar, applesauce, apple juice, and pectin for making jellies and preserves.

I left the women happily at work that morning but joined them again at the annual plant closing meeting and awards dinner. That festive affair was staged in the Gold Room of the Shenandoah Hotel on February 2, 1965. The Gold Room, the special spot for all such local festivities and events, was decorated in the Valentine motif, with flower arrangements on the tables and red hearts, candles and flowers gracing the mantel

Company officials from the Winchester headquarters attended and presented awards and special congratulations to employees having from five to as many as 30 years of service at the local plant. Betty Robinson led group singing, and Charlotte Harrison accompanied at the piano. Songs included numbers written especially for the occasion, such as "Apples," "Trimmers," "I've Been Workin' in the Apples" and "Neath the Crust of the Old Apple Pie."

Hilarity reigned supreme. Mina Nevel, the plant's own Cousin Minnie Pearl, made all of us laugh until there wasn't a dry eye in the house. The next couple, Dorothy Zombro and Anna Eaton, depicted "Sadie and Sarah," neighbors of the National Fruit Plant, and added further merriment to the program.

The jolly group joined in a hearty rendition of "Happy Birthday" for C. Lee Hammersla, one of the longtime employees. Frances Kibler was given an enthusiastic hand of applause and cheers for her decorating skill in preparing the room, then Betty Robinson closed the happy evening on a serious note by singing

"How Great Thou Art." Again, there was a note of sadness as the friends parted with promises to keep in touch.

This was National Fruit's time of busy importance in our community. The plant closed in 1984 and the late plant manager Ayres was transferred to the Winchester plant, where he worked until he retired. This brought the end of fruit processing in Martinsburg.

The National Fruit Company property was purchased in 1988 by attorney Vincent Groh of Hagerstown. In a conversation with Groh a few days ago he told me he has no immediate plans for its use. He just wants to keep it in as good condition as possible. Sections of it have been used for storage. Groh joins me in hoping proposed plans for a park in the area will materialize, and sees this project as a possibility.

But, the plant's closing brought another loss to this community. The company apparently had bought the old steamboat

Photo courtesy Berkeley County Historical Society

The National Fruit Product Company operated in Martinsburg from 1919 until its closing in 1984. At full production, the plant employed about 550 over two shift periods, with women outnumbering men four to one.

whistle that used to herald the start and end of the work day at the Auburn Wagon Works on West Race Street, and installed it at the plant, where its deep-throated sound was heard at appropriate times during the day for many years. It joined the whistles from the Interwoven and the trains on the railroad track that made each New Year's Eve such an event in those days.

These friendly voices and happy sounds come to mind today as I look upon the now-vacant National Fruit Product Company building.

I do wonder, though, what ever became of that steamboat whistle. . . .

Berkeley Woolen Mill

A busy pre-Blue Ridge Outlets industry

Adapted from ***The Journal***
2000

I shared the pleasure and anticipation of most of Martinsburg's citizens several years ago as I watched the former Berkeley Woolen Mill take on a fine, well-kept appearance with the promise of a great future as an outlet mall after Moncure Chatfield-Taylor announced his plans and began work on the buildings that had stood neglected for so many years.

I've since taken pride in the fact that it became a very attractive group of buildings and a draw for tourists to come to Martinsburg. Shortly after it opened, the company invited former employees to an open house and luncheon, where we had a nostalgic and pleasant reunion, received pins depicting the mill, and had a picture and story in *The Journal*. It was a very successful event.

Berkeley Woolen played a large part in my life. It was my dad's place of employment for 30 years. As a matter of fact, I worked there nine years, my husband worked there several years, and his mother, brother, and cousin also were employed at Berkeley Woolen at various times.

At the close of my junior year at Martinsburg High School, my dad's boss, finishing department foreman "Buddy" Brown, told him he could give me work as a "specker." My dad ran one of three shearing machines in the lower floor of the Crawford building. The weave shop was on the second floor of that building. The speckers worked across the alley in the newer Berkeley building. Our pay was 16 and a-half cents an hour or $1.65 for a 10-hour day, plus occasional overtime at straight pay.

Our pay was 16 and a-half cents an hour, or $1.65 for a 10-hour day, plus occasional overtime at straight pay.

It's important to realize that we were happy to have work, for many people didn't. We were expected to do a good job, and we gave it our best. I returned to the mill after graduating the next year, and worked in several jobs, moving from specking to "perching"—inspecting the fabric for flaws (dropped stitches) and marking them before it went to the "burlers," who mended it before it went to the washroom.

From the washroom it went through the dryer and to the large press, coming out on rollers and on to the "pencilers"—Ward Hedges, George Green, and Cecil Stuckey—who colored in the fine nubs that hadn't taken the dye. From there it went to Fred Hall at the folder, where it was folded onto bolts for the market. I later ran one of the two presses and then for my last years was a burler, which was piece work and the best-paying job for women in the finishing department.

All of my experience was in the finishing department, but the whole operation was very interesting. The factory handled the whole operation, from the huge bundles of raw wool, which was hauled to the plant by truck, through the washing, dyeing, spinning, and weaving into the finished product. I believe 400 to 450 people were employed at Berkeley Woolen Company. We made domestic fabrics, beautiful woolens for men's and women's clothing. Many people came to the mill and bought the samples that were available to the public. During World War II, blankets were made for the military, and most of the domestic work was discontinued. Guards were posted at the gate and employees wore identification tags. Dunn Woolen Mill, on the opposite side of Stephen Street, manufactured automobile upholstery, but during the war it also converted to military fabrics. That was after I left the mill in 1941.

I don't remember ever being unhappy at my work, so I'm not really aware when the strike talk began or what prompted it. Suddenly it was being whispered through the plant that we were going to strike. This was about 1934.

I remember hearing a rousing, very emotional speech by a so-called "agitator" named Hoffman, a union representative who was headquartered in Baltimore. His delivery was much like that of a television evangelist. He got all fired up, took off his coat and wiped the sweat from his brow with a bath towel.

I was no longer a specker at that time, having moved to the job of percher, which entailed pulling the cloth over my head on rollers, inspecting it by looking through it into the light of a single bulb, then marking any flaws by tying a bit of string in the selvedge. From there it went to the burlers, who sewed in the missing threads by hand. Pearl Bovey Miller was forelady of the burlers.

I was still a teenager, as was my close friend Lib (Elizabeth Pfarr Marklin), and the thought of a strike sounded like an adventure to us. We joined the union. Our only part in the strike was going down to the mill, joining the crowd watching the activities to see who went in and who didn't. Nevertheless, we were named in an injunction, but nothing ever came of it.

A bit later, we attended a meeting and were assigned to a group of coworkers who were going to Winchester to attempt to get the workers at Winchester Woolen (owned by the same company) to come out in our support. Lib and I had no idea how to approach those people, but we needn't have worried—they ignored us completely and went on their way to work. We were walking down the street when a policeman pulled up and asked what we were doing there.

Well, we were thunderstruck! We never thought of such a thing happening to us.

"We're visiting friends in Winchester," Lib replied.

"Where are you from?" the officer asked.

"Charles Town," I said quickly.

"All right!" he said. "But I know who you are, and I know what you're doing here! I'll tell you this: we've got about 15 of your buddies in jail now, and if you don't get out of town right now you'll be in there with them!"

That was all we needed. We headed out of Winchester. Just outside town, a black Packard pulled up beside us and asked if we'd like a ride. (I've always believed it was someone connected

Photo courtesy Berkeley County Historical Society

The Berkeley Woolen Mill played a large part in Ethel's life as she and several members of her family were once employed there. The mill later became a part of the Blue Ridge Outlets, a popular draw for tourists.

with the mill.) We told him we were headed home from visiting friends in Winchester and lived in Charles Town. He seemed amused, but he took us to Charles Town and let us out. Then we had to hitchhike to Martinsburg!

But the policeman knew what he was talking about. We were called "chicken" by some of our co-workers who spent the night in jail. That was the end of our strike activity, so I guess they were right. Some of the employees who were considered ring leaders were not rehired after the strike. I was among those who were and worked until 1941. Incidentally, about the mid-1930s, President Roosevelt's National Recovery Administration wage laws went into effect, and our wages were increased to 30 cents an hour and our workday reduced to eight hours. This was comparable to that paid in other local industries.

My dad, Wilbur F. Wayble, affectionately known as "Razz," worked there until the mill closed in 1948. As I said, my husband, Max D. Bovey; his mother, Annetta Hedges Bovey; his brother, Bruce Delmar Bovey; and his cousins, Bertha Hedges Armbrester, and Ward Hedges, all worked at the Berkeley Woolen Mill.

So you can see why the mill is important to me, and why I sincerely hope its future will be as bright as we anticipated a few years ago when Chatfield-Taylor announced his plans. I'd like to see the present owners take action to save the outlet mall, but if dire predictions are true, and it ceases operation, I hope some of our visionary citizens will come up with an exciting plan for use of the buildings. I'd love to be able to continue to take pride in the historic site, rather than see it fall into disrepair again.

The Martinsburg Journal

Adapted from ***The Journal***
July 9, 2000

Since I began my latest association with *The Journal,* I have been asked by present staff members what it was like working in the newsroom during my 18-year stint there (1963–1981). I'll start even before that.

This is a good time to recall an interview I had 20 years ago with Ruth B. Willey, the first woman to manage what is now the Living Section. At that time it was called Society News and she was known as society editor. However, our interview brought out the fact that there was much more to the job than her title indicated.

"If I just could have kept all my notes," she exclaimed, referring to her 40 years at the desk, "I could write a book!"

But *The Journal* was only a part of her interesting life. Her story includes a great deal of local history.

I was impressed by her sharp memory and her crisp, unhesitating manner of speaking, in view of age (she was 83 when I talked with her and at that time I thought 83 was quite old). She graduated in 1915 from the old Martinsburg High School, presently the School Administration Building at the corner of Stephen and South Queen streets. Shortly after that she accepted her first job, setting up a card file at the Old National Bank on the Public Square, now One Valley Bank. After only a few weeks, she went to work at the Court House, where the Berkeley County Health Department was located. She found that interesting work.

"Dr. W. T. Henshaw, who was later to become state health commissioner, was head of the department," she says, "and our offices were on the top floor. One of the things I remember best was that Dr. Henshaw made a personal inspection of every school in the county each spring—and I went along. I'll never forget, we had to drive up a dry creek bed in Back Creek Valley to get to one little school!"

About that time, she said, there was "some agitation" for establishment of a farm bureau, and after a lot of official visiting back and forth, presumably from Charleston, an office was opened in Martinsburg and she went to work for the Berkeley County Farm Bureau. The first man in charge was a Professor Dorsey from West Virginia University, and the next was Carl Beebe—a big, pleasant, round-faced man, whom she said they used to call the Mellon's Food Baby—but not to his face.

Photo from Journal article

Ruth Willey

Those two were followed by Carl Degen and Dick Greenland, both from Huntingdon, Pennsylvania. The latter joined one of the limestone companies and remained here until his death.

The first permanent agent was W. M. Bewick. Paul Teal came next, and it was during Teal's tenure in 1923, that Miss Willey left and went to work for *The Journal*. This was before the days of titles or specialization of the job.

"I did everything but sports," she said firmly. "I handled county correspondence, wrote deaths, read proof and I was society editor. I handled all incoming telephone calls, too. We worked six days a week, and we didn't have air conditioning. We worked until the water dripped off our elbows!

"Frances Townsend was business manager in the front office,

and Gilbert McKown was editor. Max Von Schlegel owned the paper at that time. *The Journal* and *The Evening World* had just consolidated, and shortly after that, Von Schlegel sold out to the Ogden Newspapers."

Vernon Garton had come to Martinsburg as first editor of *The Journal* with its founder, Harry F. Byrd Sr., who later became U.S. Senator from Virginia. When *The Journal* and *The World* consolidated, Garton had yielded that position to McKown and "taken to the street" as roving reporter, covering the news beat.

The Journal at that time had only one room, which is now occupied by the Display Advertising Department, said Willey. The C&P Telephone Company's operation was on the second floor of the building. Brownie Thompson was telegraph operator. The news came in by telegraph in code, and he transcribed it on a typewriter in one corner of the room. This system pre-dated the teletype. Willey's first assignment was to cover a Women's Club meeting in Shepherdstown. Brand new on the job, she didn't even drive a car, and at the time of our interview had no recollection of how she got back and forth, but she followed through.

The emphasis at that time, as it continued to be while I was on the job, was on local news, and she had to keep an ear tuned to events of interest.

"I went to work at 8 A.M. and I'd get on the line and call key women about social events. There were certain women who would tell me when anyone was having something," she explained.

The Journal published two editions. The first went out about 2:30 P.M. to Jefferson and Morgan Counties, and the 4 o'clock edition was for local subscribers. A special edition was put out at the time of President Franklin D. Roosevelt's death, April 12, 1945. Everything Miss Willey wrote had to cross the desk of Editor McKown, and she called him "a rigid taskmaster." He often challenged her use of words, and being the authority, he always came out the victor—a fact stifling to any writer.

Then came the memorable day when Austin Wood, publisher for the Ogden group, stopped by her desk and said, "Miss Willey, from now on, you are on your own."

"From that time on it was a real pleasure!" she declared. "That changed my whole feeling about it, and permitted more self-expression and more comfort in my work. I believe too, that was when I began to write my own headlines."

She reported having very few unpleasant experiences in her work, but did recall one instance when she picked up the wedding of a local couple from an out-of-town paper, called the bride's mother for more information and was forbidden to use the story.

She stayed on the job one year after the usual retirement age in order to round out 40 years, retiring in May 1963 at the age of 66. (I thought that was a pretty good age then, little realizing I later would retire at age 66 and consider it early retirement.) That was the month I was offered the job, and it was the dream I'd had for years.

Photo from Journal article

Paul Buxton (Buck) Martin

I didn't know until some time later that she had recommended me to follow in her footsteps because she liked my work. I had done publicity many years for groups of which I was a member, as well as for my church, my family and, in fact at any opportunity. Paul Buxton (Buck) Martin, a classmate of mine, had become editor in 1962 upon the retirement of

Gilbert McKown, and it was he who offered me the position of society editor. Without a day's journalism training, but a lifelong love of writing, I accepted without hesitation and learned on the job.

Buck encouraged freedom of expression, but expected accuracy, especially where names were concerned. He reminded me that news is not written just for today, but that newspapers keep "morgues" that are used as references for historians, so accuracy is essential and corrections come late. Things hadn't changed a great deal in some respects when I started to work. The paper had grown a lot, but each member of the news staff learned how to do everyone else's job. When our work was caught up, we were expected to help at the proof desk. That was considered a very responsible job, and existed until computers were brought in about the late '70s or early '80s.

During my early years there, I still had the responsibility of answering the telephone, and knowing what was going on in clubs and organizations was an important part of the job. People brought in stories of events or we covered them. Anyone was free to walk in to see any editor: Those affiliated with sports came in to talk with Sports Editor Bob Scrivener, people in law enforcement came in to see George Gutsell, and local and state officials came in to talk to Buck. He often brought them around to our desks and introduced them to us. We met many prominent people that way.

Anyone who wanted me to bring my camera and cover a reception, a party, a check passing, a wedding anniversary, a church event or a special club meeting came in and we set up an appointment. I was expected to cover those activities. Of course, there were times that I covered Kiwanis, Civitan, Chamber of Commerce, or such meetings, if assigned. I loved getting out to do those things and made many friends. The stories that were brought in had to be typed and turned in to Bill Thompson, managing editor. We each had a camera and turned our film over to

George Gutsell, or later to Pat Dockeney, now editor of the *Spirit of Jefferson* in Charles Town, for processing. However, news for my page was not sent through anyone else but was solely my responsibility.

Birthday parties, family reunions, and all of what I call "people" events, were viewed as important local news. Names were always considered news, and all who attended such events were listed. Many times, I listed 100 or more names in a family reunion story, and if I missed Aunt Mary's name I heard about it and followed with an apology and a correction.

Many times, in those pre-computer days, I brought home reunions or weddings to type on a Sunday afternoon and turn in Monday morning. Our deadline was 10 A.M. for the current day's edition. I was happy when the News for Women, as I had christened it, became an advance page. It took some of the pressure off.

The dummy pages, advertising spaces laid out, were brought in and distributed, and we put them on our desk, got out our ruler and a pencil with a good eraser, and laid out our stories, writing our own headlines. We each had what we called a "wheel" to gauge the size we wanted our pictures enlarged or reduced to and indicated cropping with crop lines. If there was a problem in the paste-up department downstairs we might get a call from Mike Allen or Margie Hess asking for help in getting the effect we wanted. Sometimes we stood beside them until the work was completed. There was real cooperation and teamwork.

We had what were known as "outlying correspondents." Those women collected news from their particular areas, such as Ganotown, Hedgesville, Marlowe, Jones Spring, and sections of Jefferson County. They painstakingly wrote it down on ledger sheets and mailed it in. This all had to be typed and turned in to the teletype operators, Jane Weller and Doris McDonald. For some years this was part of my work.

Faye LaBeau handled local news and obituaries. The latter were brought by or called in from the funeral homes. Occasionally, she went out on assignments. When Faye resigned, Peggy May (now McClurken) came in to handle women's news and promptly renamed the section the "Family Pages." Anna Catherine Hare took over most of the typing and handled the obituaries after we went to computers and proofreading was discontinued.

I was named feature editor and was given a pretty free hand to do what I wanted. I had written a column, "At Our House..." for some years, and ventured into editorial comment and thought-provoking features as well as highlighting local people. It brought me great pleasure to give someone "a day in the sun." I loved it all.

Fred and Maxine Newbraugh handled the news from Berkeley Springs and Morgan County for 27 years and turned it in by telephone and in writing. They covered sports, automobile accidents, elections, street fights, obituaries, and all sorts of news for

Photo from Journal article

Members of *The Journal* newsroom staff in the late 1960s or early '70s gathered around the proof desk. From left, Anna Catherine Hare, proofreader; Faye LaBeau, local news reporter; Sarah Snyder, Jefferson County reporter.

that county. Sarah Snyder joined the staff in 1964 and handled Jefferson County news.

That's when the Jefferson County Bureau opened. State and national news came in by teletype, and I well remember November 22, 1963, the day President Kennedy was assassinated. Bells on the teletype rang insistently to signal important news, and Bill Thompson hurried over to see what was going on. We were all in shock. Everything stopped as we waited to hear what the final outcome would be before going to press. Then we learned the President was dead. It was a sad day, one that will live in memory.

I'm not sure when we changed to the process known as offset printing, but we had that in place for some time before the computers came in. I was a bit scared when Page Burdette, who became editor after Buck Martin retired, came in and set a terminal on my desk and carried away the old typewriter I'd been using. He gave minimal instruction with a few notes and told us to take over and learn to use the computer. We did, and I loved it after I caught on and missed it dreadfully when I retired.

Another day stands out in my memory. George Gutsell's police scanner crackled out the news that a state policeman had been shot in Morgan County, and George scurried out, camera in hand. A short time later, the scanner brought in news of a bank holdup in Winchester, adding that the two suspects were headed north on Route 11 toward Martinsburg. With George out of the office, there was no one available to send out on that story. Anna Catherine knew a shortcut she thought the men might take, so she and Peggy were dispatched to track down the robbers. Fortunately, our family page editor and proofreader arrived just as the two men were taken into custody by officers. So they saved the day. *The Journal* was represented at the scene.

Although this was a memorable occasion, Anna Catherine always said her favorite memory was of the day Buck took her to the airport to meet Ronald Reagan, whom she had always admired, when he was a candidate for President and stopped off in Martinsburg.

Liz Thompson, now with the Hagerstown *Morning Herald,* held the position of family editor for a time while I was there as did Kathleen Linger. Nancy Miller served as a reporter and helped with special sections at various times during her high school and college days.

We considered ourselves a small town newspaper with a mission to provide a service to the community and warmth that we hoped would permeate the area.

Like Ruth Willey, I enjoyed my work at *The Journal.* We were like family. We set up a table and brought in cakes to celebrate our birthdays, we decorated the newsroom for holidays, and we really cared about each other. We had occasional picnics. My husband Max and I had staff members out to our home to picnic on the patio and watch the fireworks at the park one Fourth of July. Once, we went to the Bavarian Inn for dinner. We considered ourselves a small town newspaper with a mission to provide a service to the community and warmth that we hoped would permeate the area. I think we succeeded.

I remember that we once learned that a gentle, older pastor of one of the smaller churches had a birthday coming up. When he brought in his next weekly church notice, we were ready for him with a decorated birthday cake and heartfelt greetings. There were tears in his eyes and ours, too.

But, we're not a small town any more. As in so many cases, for everything we gain we also lose a little something. So, *The Journal* I worked for has grown along with the town and in growing, it has gained sophistication and left behind some of what I loved. No, we cannot go back to the small town paper any more than we can go back to the small town we once knew, and I'm not sure we'd want to. But it's nice to remember both occasionally.

After all this reminiscing, I want to add that my present association with *The Journal* is refreshing and a joy. I have the greatest admiration for my friend Maria Lorensen as editor and for the young people on her staff who also have become my friends. They have earned degrees in journalism and are on their way up in their chosen careers.

We were local people who had learned on the job and were happy to remain where we were, in our hometown. They, in turn, will be here for a while, then move on as opportunity beckons. May God's blessings and our fondest wishes be with them while they are with us and always. I hope their memories of Martinsburg and their work at *The Journal* will be happy ones.

Philosophy, Faith, Love

Never Too Old to Learn

Think of life as one long lesson

Adapted from ***The Journal***
August 22, 1999

You're younger today than you'll ever be again. You've no doubt heard that old axiom many times, but it's never so true as when considering education. It's so easy to tell yourself you really missed the boat—that the biggest mistake you ever made was not finishing high school, going to college, studying math or even just leaning to type—whatever it might be that you feel has held you back from realizing your potential.

There was a time when this was excusable, but no longer. Any course under the sun that you might want to try is available in the hundreds of adult education opportunities offered in Berkeley County or at one of the nearby colleges, all at little cost.

For some years I regretted not having studied typing in high school. Then I read a motivational book. I'm not even sure of the title—but its message struck home. Somewhere within its pages I found just the incentive I needed. It told me NEVER to say, "I wish I had done this or that." Just get busy and do it.

I did it, and that move made it possible for me to write—the work I've done practically all my life. I had some work published in poetry publications and in-house journals. Prior to that time, much of what I'd done, hunt-and-peck on a borrowed antique typewriter, had never seen the light of day except for sharing it with friends.

Martinsburg Business College, which had closed some years before, reopened and I had the opportunity to study typing. I enrolled and was the oldest member of the class at the age of 41. Not many people were returning to school at that time. Others in the class were young people and some veterans who were studying under the GI Bill.

This was 1956—and I had graduated from Martinsburg High School in 1932. It was fun being the oldest in the class. It was most interesting, and although the school was closed a few months later, I had a handwritten note from the teacher, Mrs. Edna Winfrey, that confirmed that I had done satisfactorily.

I applied for work as a clerk in an insurance claims office, was hired, and worked there six years, which gave me time to learn more about typing and office procedure. Then one day, heaven opened up!

I met a classmate, Paul B. "Buck" Martin at the post office and he asked me if I'd like to work in the newsroom at *The Journal*. He hired me at the age of 47, with only a love for words and a great respect for a well-turned phrase but not a day's training in journalism. He said he felt I could learn on the job, and he trained me. How I loved the freedom to write what I wished, expressed the way I wanted to express it. Well, for the next 18 years that's what I did, and it added a new dimension to my life.

Then came the computer age. I was still writing, of course, although I'd left the newspaper in 1981. I had a typewriter with word-processing capability. I was 80 when my daughter Sharilyn decided to upgrade her computer system and asked if I'd like to have hers. Of course I accepted. She taught me to make greeting cards, posters and such things.

I enjoyed it so much that for my 81st birthday I got a new computer, then enrolled in an Adult Education computer class—again the oldest in the class! *The Journal's* own Lou Ramos was the instructor. It was really cool! We had a ball. At the close of the class I took photos of the class members—we were all over 55—

Photo from Journal article

Ethel at her typewriter at *The Journal* shortly after going to work for the newspaper in the 1960s She credits taking a typing class at age 41 with launching her dream career in journalism. Still later, at age 81, she enrolled in a computer class and entered into yet another era of writing.

and made up a little "yearbook" with a class song and everything. It was all in fun, of course.

Now, here I am again, writing occasionally for *The Journal* and enjoying it immensely. I'll never set the world on fire and I'm no real threat to famous writers, but I'm certainly enjoying this. I've had several things published over the years—mostly verse—but the newspaper has always been my favorite outlet. I've met so many interesting people and made friends that have enriched my life—just because in the beginning I decided to go back to school! I've even been invited to give motivational talks to older people.

Nothing is quite so crippling as living in a closed world of your own making, imprisoned by bonds of a mind that has stopped growing and learning.

I heard a very wise man say that a mind once stretched to accommodate a new idea never shrinks back to its original size again. I believe this. Nothing is quite so crippling as living in a closed world of your own making, imprisoned by bonds of a mind that has stopped growing and learning. So think about it.

Remember, you'll never again be as young as you are today!

The Other Side of the Coin

Adapted from ***The Journal***
February 23, 2003

As a reader of my columns, you know I tell (or share) many of the experiences of my life, so you may find it difficult to believe that I'm a rather private person in some respects. However, recent events and comments I've read and heard from others have prompted me to open my heart concerning a very personal experience.

This is the 20th anniversary of the *Roe vs. Wade* decision that established the legality of abortion. Opinions both pro and con have come from all sides, from syndicated columnists to letters to the editor. I'd like to give the viewpoint of one who yearned for years to become a mother, only to keep losing one child after another by what I prefer to call miscarriage, rather than the medical term "spontaneous abortion."

My point in coming forth with my story is to correct the impression that pro-choice advocates give, intentionally or thoughtlessly, but certainly not accurately. That is, that an abortion is just ridding a woman's body of an unwanted blob of tissue and blood that, if left intact, would, in a few months, suddenly take the form of a baby. This is what they would have you believe.

My friend, that is not the case. Take it from one who has seen and mourned the loss of little ones who had occupied the womb only four or five months—these are indeed babies. They are perfectly formed, doll-sized little people, outwardly lacking only fingernails, toenails and eyelashes. Their hairlines are distinct, their tiny ears are perfectly formed, and their miniature faces mirror the features of their parents. Were it not for the heartbreak suffered in the loss, these infants are marvelous to behold.

This comes from one who, with aching heart, has seen these little ones dressed in doll-size clothing and laid to rest in the cemetery. I have friends who have shared the same experience.

These babies were formed and grew in the shelter of the mother's womb, completely innocent of their precarious position and what might lie ahead for them. Would they remain to mature, then come into the world to be loved and nurtured as the Lord intended, or would they be lost prematurely by miscarriage—or, worse yet, forcibly removed by abortion?

My experience long pre-dated modern technology, so I never saw my little ones while they were developing and never enjoyed

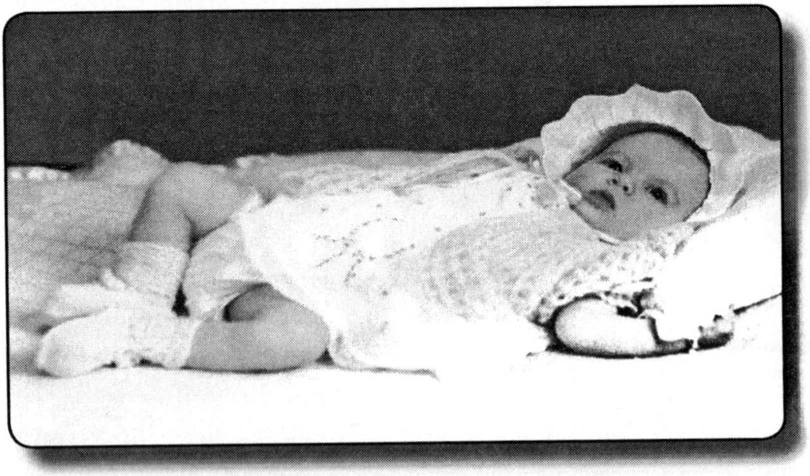

Photo by Gerbrick from author's collection

After years of grief and disappointment, Ethel and husband Max were blessed with the birth of a much-loved daughter. Baby Sharilyn is pictured above.

watching them during those months they were a part of me. But I did feel their movements, I did learn to love them, and I did plan joyfully for their arrival. Then, invariably, would come the day when I knew it was all over. The grief and disappointment were overwhelming for me, for my husband who shared my eagerness to be a parent, and our families as well.

Well-meaning friends, wanting to be sympathetic, said things like, "Well, it was probably for the best. There might have been something wrong with it." Or, "You're young. You can have another one." Or, cheerfully, "Well, you'll just have to try again!" Please, don't ever say things like that! It's enough just to offer a hug and say, "I'm so sorry."

I'm glad to say my own story has a very happy ending. Our happiness knew no bounds the day we were finally blessed with the birth of a much-loved daughter who has been a real joy through the years.

But I want to set the record straight—the abortionist's tool is not removing a lifeless hunk of fetal matter. It is giving pain and death to a real baby who suffers in silence, who could bring joy into someone's home if given the opportunity to live—and just maybe grow up to be a productive citizen.

Pray about it.

Please Don't Tamper With My Beliefs

Adapted from ***The Journal***
October 3, 1999

Every now and then through the years, we seem to get into a situation in which we must defend our faith and try to convince someone why we feel as we do, worship as we choose, or teach our children as we wish.

We get into long debates, verbal and otherwise, that do little to help matters, but cause ill feelings—and take up space in the newspaper that could be used to better advantage. This is the way I see the present arguments about the Ten Commandments and the teaching of evolution vs. creation in public schools.

We who are believers feel a need to convert others to our way of thinking, and apparently those who are not believers are determined to try to blast our faith in one way or another. This is a debate without limit. I just want to defend my right to hold onto the faith that is precious to me.

I am thankful that we are a country founded on a trust in God. It is engraved in all our coins and emblazoned on many of our public buildings. Despite the efforts of the atheists to take this fact away from us, in times of strife or disaster, it brings special comfort to our hearts.

Whenever we are threatened by hard times or national and international crises, one can sense a need on the part of most people to feel closer to a Supreme Being. Even those who are usually filled with self-reliance, who claim to need no one, change a bit at times like those or during religious holidays.

I often wonder how it would be to profess no belief, to scoff at such a thing. What would we do when we face sorrow, or a problem too great to solve by our own initiative? Where would we turn when someone dear to us is taken away? Or when tragedy strikes and sorrow settles over our hearts and fills us with despair?

Can you imagine the emptiness, the utter hopelessness?

What would we do when the sunrise seen from the kitchen window is almost too beautiful to bear? Or when someone who has been so ill that there seems no hope at all suddenly looks up with recognition in his eyes? Whom would we thank?

How would it be to have no one to thank when you look for the first time into the tiny, new, yet somehow familiar, face of your own newborn baby? It seems to me that having no one to thank would be nearly as bad as having no one to lean on when sorrow fills the heart.

If suddenly we were to be forbidden by law to pray—even a simple "Thank You, God! Thank You!"—would we value the privilege more?

But one of the greatest blessings is the fact that the mind and heart are always free. No one can legislate our thoughts and our feelings. The greatest power on earth cannot forbid my mind to praise the Lord or my heart to love and worship Him. Nor can the words of derision spoken or written by unbelievers have the slightest bearing on my faith.

I believe that my Lord meant it when he said to Martha, "Whosoever liveth and believeth in me shall never die." And again when He said to the thief on the cross, "Today thou shall be with me in paradise."

I believe that eternal life begins when we accept Him as our Lord and that my loved ones go from my arms to His. This faith has meant a great deal to me through the years, so I say to those who scoff, please don't tamper with my beliefs.

In the meantime, let's get about the business of trying to do our best for each other here on earth. Then, if one day the Lord should say to me, "Ethel, the earthly life is all I had for you," I shall say, "Thank You, Lord. I loved it and gave it my best."

Living a New Role

Adapted from ***The Journal***
February 27, 2000

I am learning to live in a different world—the world of the woman on her own. This role has been thrust upon me by the hands of time, just as it has upon many women before me. My husband Max passed away the day before Christmas, 1999.

Friends and family have been wonderful support, and I have been surrounded and comforted by their care and concern, but my daily life has changed in so many ways. It's the small things you miss—talking over the events of the day, sharing your thoughts.

So I would like to tell you something about the man whose life I shared for 62 years. We were married December 4, 1937, in the midst of the Great Depression. We'd known each other in school for some years before we decided we'd like to be more than friends. Then we had a four-year courtship before we had the courage to take the leap into marriage.

We drove to Ellerslie, Maryland, in Max's 1931 Chevrolet Coupe, expecting to be married by a young pastor who had been his classmate at Shepherd College. It turned out that he had been transferred to a church in another town, and an older man was serving that church. He had just come in from hunting, gun in hand, and we waited while he changed his clothes.

Then he married us in the parlor with his wife as the only

Photo from author's collection

Max and Ethel as newlyweds. They were married in 1937 in the midst of the Great Depression in what Max later described as "the next thing to a shotgun wedding." The preacher had just come in from hunting, gun in hand.

witness. When Max told the story, he always said it was the next thing to a shotgun wedding—and the preacher had the gun.

We drove to nearby Cumberland and stopped at Max's Aunt Ruth Shriver's home. She insisted upon serving us our first meal as husband and wife—a veal steak dinner. That was in 1937, and Aunt Ruth lived to be 109 years old!

We stayed overnight at the Francis Scott Key Hotel in Frederick, then went on to Washington the following day to visit my Aunt Bess and Uncle Ed Hill. We attended a show at the Fox Theater and headed for home as the snow began to fall. Both my uncle and aunt are gone now, but Aunt Bess always thought Max looked like Robert Taylor, a popular actor of the time.

He was handsome, had curly black hair and brown eyes, a keen sense of humor and a terrific personality, all things I particularly admired. Besides, I knew and loved his mother and the other members of his family, so we had a great start for a good marriage. One of the nicest compliments I ever had came years later, when his mother said, "Max married Ethel—and she's good for a lifetime!"

Our first home was a three-room apartment. We ordered a breakfast set from Wards and it was six weeks arriving. In the meantime we used a card table borrowed from our landlady, Katherine Campion, county health nurse. I sat on the clothes hamper and Max sat in the window sill as we enjoyed our meals.

After the furniture arrived, the clothes hamper was moved to the living room, where it became a table to hold the lamp beside our one lounge chair, which, with a sofa and radio, completed our furniture for that room until, one piece at a time, we furnished the apartment. We lived there three years.

We both worked at the Berkeley Woolen Mill—I from 7 A.M. to 4 P.M. and he from 4 P.M. to midnight. I napped after work so we could have time together when he came home. When he later went on day shift, it was great.

We were delighted when we could move into a six-room house with three porches at 320 South Tennessee Avenue in 1943, and that was our home for eight years. By that time our much-yearned-for daughter had joined us and we wanted our own home.

We went shopping for a piece of land we could afford. The Rosemont Company had a large plat showing lots at the outskirts of town, an area beginning at Tennessee Avenue and going westward. At that time this was undeveloped, having been mostly farmland.

Max and I, his sister Dot and her husband, George Miller, went out together and chose adjoining lots. As I recall, ours cost $550. Dot and George immediately selected a pre-cut house from the Aladdin Homes catalog and hired George Dodge, a carpenter friend, to build it. There was no city water, no garbage service, no electricity, nor even a street through to the lots. Each of these utilities had to be obtained by a trip to proper authorities. In fact, the mayor complained loudly about these people who wanted to build in the country but have all of the city services.

We looked in a book from Berkeley Lumber Company, found the plan we wanted, and I was sent to talk with the lumber company owner, Roderick Cheeseman, himself a local developer, to get an estimate. He set me back on my heels with this comment, "You realize you're talking about a house in the $20,000 range."

Well, I certainly did NOT realize that. This was 1949, when nice homes were being built for $4,000 and $5,000, and really fine ones might cost $10,000. In fact, we had a book on the shelf at home called, "How to Build Your Dream Home for $3,500." It's still there.

Typically, Max didn't consider making another choice. He never believed in spending money he didn't have, but he never liked to settle for less than he wanted, and we wanted that house. He started looking for friends who had the knowledge or talent he needed and he resolved to serve as his own contractor.

The first of these was "Mister Billy" Thompson who, I believe, turned the first shovelful of dirt for the footer, the trench to be filled with concrete upon which the foundation would be laid. I don't know how many people worked on that footer, but "Mister Billy" was only the first. Max worked alongside them after a full day's work at Fairchild in Hagerstown and a side job as an auto mechanic in a garage in his mother's backyard, where he also repaired bicycles and sold and mounted Whizzer bike motors.

After the foundation was added came the sealing and more work. My dad, whom Max lovingly called "Pap," (my dad's choice) helped apply the sealing. This was a mixture of tar and something else painted on with a brush to make it waterproof. My dad didn't live to see the house completed. I remember the day, much later, when Max came home after the bulldozer had filled in at the back of the house. "Well, the last of Pap's work was covered up today," he said, with a catch in his voice.

The concrete siding blocks were laid by Frank Leonard. Then Minghini Contractors were hired to put the house under roof so the inside work could begin. Here again came the willing hands of friends, including Floyd Johnston and his father-in-law, Amos Minnich. Later, Rex Rinker was hired to do the fine interior work. Max worked alongside them and learned a great deal about a line of work he'd never explored. He laid flooring, nailed plasterboard (he'd long before decided he wanted the walls plastered), and learned how to hang windows and trim window and door frames.

Our landlady raised our rent from $25 a month to a hefty $40. We decided we could use that extra $15 for materials for our house. So we moved into our far-from-completed home in March 1951.

Then the unexpected happened. Our landlady raised our rent from $25 a month to a hefty $40. We decided we could use that extra $15 for materials for our house. So we moved into our far-from-completed home in March 1951. The rain poured that first day. Max was unable to help in the move because he was having a bad time and almost flat on his back with Osteoarthritis, a condition that was to continue in varying degrees from that time on. (In later years, Max had three back operations and a hip replacement.) His brother Leon helped out that day.

The movers carried our furniture into the house from the back patio door into the living room because that was the only available entry. Three concrete blocks were the only way to reach the front door, and the door into the kitchen was many feet above the ground at that side of the house, where the dirt hadn't been filled in. As soon as he set down his load, the first man exclaimed in surprise, "Why, this house isn't finished!"

I looked around me at the unfinished floor, the unframed windows where I had used thumbtacks to hang bright flowered plastic curtains, and the plaster-splashed roughed-in stairway the builders had put in for their own use while working on the second floor, and wondered how he could tell so soon. I eagerly started placing the furniture according to the sketches I'd made on graph sheets during the many months I was waiting and thought I was one of the luckiest people in the world. And I was—because I was happy.

Work continued. The hardwood flooring was laid, the windows and doors were framed, doorsills were put in place, steps replaced the ladder that led to the basement, a hearth was laid and a mantel was placed in the living room. I remember four-year-old Sharilyn coming home from her playmate Kathy Simmons' home, quite impressed. "They even have carpet sills!" she exclaimed.

So it went. Each little necessity had its turn at being a luxury. Hard work, sore muscles, and determination slowly paid off as the house gradually took shape, and we were proud of the accomplishment.

We had nearly 50 years together in our home, gardening and working through the years. Some were a little leaner than others, but it was a good, satisfying time. Our daughter, our pride and joy, has brought us much happiness. We were blessed indeed.

The past several years brought physical problems, but the man I married continued to manifest his God-given personality. He never developed an invalid personality or a "poor me" attitude despite his pain, but worked hard and led an active life. There were times during the early part of his last illness that weakness and medication took their toll.

But, I'm happy to say the loving care he received in the hos-

Photo from author's collection

Ethel and Max relaxing at home with their little dog Rascal in later years. Max passed away in December 1999 after 62 years of marriage.

pital and after returning home restored him to more of his former self than any of us had ever dreamed possible. He had two years of grace, two years to enjoy his home, to go out to the garage and putter, to talk to friends who dropped in, and to enjoy his little dog, Rascal, who spent many happy hours with him in his lift chair, sharing the warmth and closeness.

Then, in mid-December, he contracted a cold or virus that led to pneumonia and thence to congestive heart failure, and after 10 days in intensive care, he breathed his last on earth and went to his reward.

I haven't made an effort to give you his life story, his various interests, his love of travel, his pleasure in his family, working with the Masons, his work at Fairchild during World War II and later at Capitol Cement Corporation, where he retired from in 1977. But his lodge brothers, former coworkers, other friends and relatives, and even the nurses who had grown to know him, had praise for him and tears in their eyes as they brought comfort to the family with interesting and humorous anecdotes about their association with him.

I just wanted to tell you a little about the person he was. He was a good man, a good husband and father, and he touched many lives. I pray our lives will reflect his enthusiasm, his faith, courage, and positive attitude as the legacy he left to us, along with many happy memories.

Self-Perception

*Adapted from **The Journal***
September 23, 2002

I was being interviewed by a Shepherd College nursing student, and we were nearing the close of the session when she asked the most probing question of the afternoon.

"How do you perceive yourself?"

Her blue eyes gazed intently into mine as she sat, pen poised over her note pad, waiting for my response.

Well! How do I perceive myself? I'm not sure I'd ever asked myself that question. I finally said that I saw myself as a woman who had lived a long life with joys and sorrows and with many blessings, but I felt the Lord must have something He wants me to do because I'm still here. I was sincere, and didn't intend it as a flip reply. But her question has given me much pause for thought in the months since our interview.

I believe we need to ask ourselves that searching question many times in our lifetime. Our self-perception can change with the choices we make and the consequences of those choices. Things that happen to us, good or bad, and our response to those things change us, for better or for worse. They bring out our qualities, our strengths and weaknesses, our inner goodness and selfishness, our pride and humility.

In short, life's experiences and our circumstances have helped to mold us into the people we have become, and if we never take a step back, figuratively, and look at ourselves, we don't really know who we are! Not learning that would be an irreparable loss. We must define who we are, for our peace of mind.

There is a certain strength gained by self-analysis, a certain self-confidence. I know nothing about psychology, so I speak only from my own feelings and limited experience. I said we must define ourselves, but I have found that this is a continuing process. As our circumstances change, we must redefine ourselves again and again.

As our circumstances change, we must redefine ourselves again and again.

The thing we must not do, for our own mental and physical health, is perceive ourselves as lesser persons because of changes in our situation. With the passing years, of course we find we can do fewer and fewer of the things we once did. But this does not mean that we are worthless, that our words have no meaning, that our opinion has no value, or that nobody cares what we think or do!

Don't let this negative attitude take over your life! Don't let it affect your persona. Be the person you are, regardless. I have friends who are a real inspiration to me, who have followed this line of reasoning successfully for years. I've learned from them how to accept my losses and my limitations and move on to live my life. I cannot let circumstances dictate my perception of myself as a person.

Several years ago, things began happening to me that I'd never anticipated. Osteoarthritis entered the scene. Foot and leg problems began affecting my gait, making my walk unsteady. Naturally, this led to falls, with no really serious injuries except to my pride. Someone suggested that I use a cane.

A cane? Me?

Then I began noticing people who carried a cane for support, and I started thinking it might not be such a bad idea. But I didn't follow the suggestion. That is, I didn't until I fell and fractured a hip, leading to hip replacement.

Replaced knees followed (not the result of falls) and surgery on three vertebrae. Then, I fell and fractured a lumbar vertebra and there was no question but that I needed assistance in walking. A cane wouldn't do now—I needed more support. A walker needed to be lifted and set down at every step. It hurt my back and really didn't fit my lifestyle. Then a dear friend found the perfect solution—a three-wheel walker that has opened up my world again! It's my constant companion and a blessing.

The walker cannot be used on stairs, so next came a ramp, from my back porch to the patio leading to the garage. This enables me to reach the van, lift the walker in behind the driver's seat, and take off! My declaration of independence!

How do I perceive myself now? No doubt strangers see the walker before they see me, but it has become a part of my identity—a sort of "love me, love my walker." I see it as an extension of myself, and so do my friends. And my life goes on—happily.

My daughter and my friends are real blessings in my life, but I'm able to do many things for myself, such as writing this column for the paper and giving motivational talks to other people of seasoned age.

Now let me tell you about the friends whose example inspired me. We are in a Sunday School class of extraordinary women. We enjoy each other's company and are a real support group, and I could write a story about each member. But I chose just three.

The first is Elizabeth Rife, a friend since Hooge Street School days. Liz was born physically impaired and spent many months in a body cast and years after that seeking help for her condition with limited success. But has this deterred her from living an active life? Far from it! She ran her own beauty shop for years, married, has three grown children, grandchildren, and great-grandchildren, and she is one of those women envied by many for her ability to plan and organize activities in her church, then work to help carry them out. She has a lively personality and boundless energy. Her secret? "I do whatever I have to do to get done what I want to get done!" she declares.

Liz loves being outdoors, especially fishing. She drives her car and never turns down an opportunity to go somewhere—such as her trip to Germany to visit her grandson who's in the military service. I'm not sure Germany was ready for that invasion, but she had a memorable visit. A walker is the basis of her independence.

Another of my friends since childhood is Carrie Starliper. Arthritis is at the root of her problem, plus some neural surgery. She is a cancer survivor and participates in the annual walk and program. She carries a cane to help in her walking. She too is active in the class, has served as president and vice-president, visits shut-ins and doesn't let her difficulties get her down. Carrie also has a grown family, a son and twin daughters, six grandchildren and one great-grandchild.

Eloise Knaggs, who until recently served as longtime president of the class, is the other of my remarkable friends. She has a bubbling personality and a never-give-up philosophy. She has had much sorrow in her life, surgery and other serious physical problems, but you'd never see it in her smile. On the contrary, she's willing and eager to lend a hand wherever she can, loves to visit shut-ins and takes part in all activities. Last year, she flew to Australia to visit her granddaughter who was there as an exchange student and gained friends, who were her granddaughter's hosts. She never mentions the fact that because of her emphysema she is on oxygen every night. Eloise also is a mother, grandmother and great-grandmother.

After longtime marriages, all four of us are now "singles,"

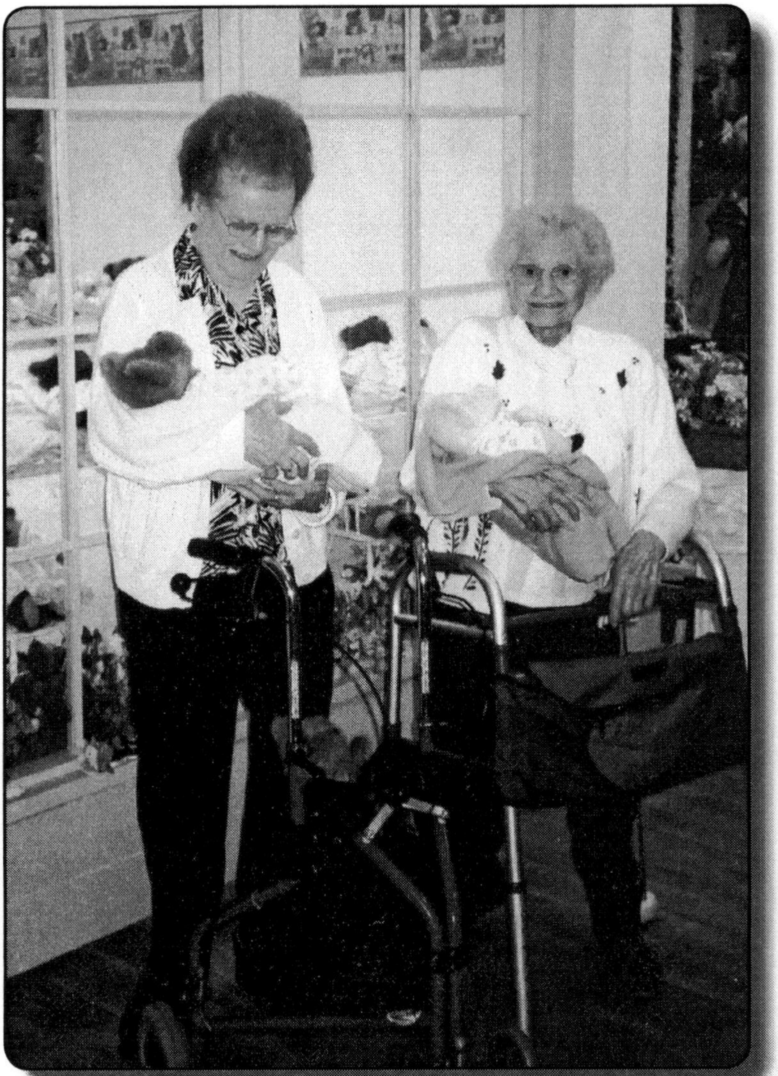

Photo from author's collection

Ethel, left, and her long-time friend Elizabeth Rife, holding baby bears from the nursery during a visit to Boyds Bear Country in Gettysburg, Pennsylvania. Liz, says Ethel, is one of several friends who inspire her. Both credit their walkers with giving them independence.

today's politically correct term for widows. Whatever you choose to call us, we're on our own, but in every case we perceive ourselves as women who have a zest for life, a purpose in living, and look forward to every tomorrow as a promise of something worthwhile. We are blessed with friends and family who love and accept us as we are, contributing to our sense of pride in our personhood. However, the tremendously important factor in our life is the inner joy that comes only with complete faith in God.

A special value in learning to perceive ourselves as worthwhile individuals is that it opens our hearts to others in situations similar to our own. We learn to look beyond the cane, the walker, or the wheelchair for the bright eyes or the smile that lights up a face. We offer a cheery greeting and more often than not receive one in return. Even if we don't, our words and our smile still may have added a bit of brightness to someone's day.

How thankful I am that the nursing student asked the question that led me to this important search! Thank you, Lauron!

Afterword

Celebrating 70 Years

The preparation of this book for publication has truly been a stroll down Memory Lane for me. While much has been said about the evolution of Martinsburg, *Hometown Memories* is about the professional growth and personal development of individuals as well. On this note, I would like to close with a bit of high school reminiscing and a salute to some special people I have had the privilege of knowing.

In May 2002, I and 13 other surviving members of the Martinsburg High School class of 1932 got together to celebrate our 70-year class reunion with an afternoon of dining and fun. Some came with canes, some with walkers, some in wheelchairs, but the one thing all had in common was a sparkle in their eyes when they spotted each other and a smile and handshake or a hug to share. The group is not large, but their pleasure in being together never wavers from year to year.

The Ricochet Quartet—Frank Bradley, Dave Lasko, Kenny Floyd and John Fisher—resplendent in blue shirts with red, white, and blue neckties, gave a concert of barbershop quartet music, adding jokes and banter to their presentation to the delight of their listeners. They dedicated a number to Frances Keller, a class member celebrating her 87th birthday. Frances gave piano lessons in Martinsburg for many years.

Donald Hill traveled the longest distance of any class member to attend the reunion, coming from Hampstead, Maryland, and bringing three guests.

Photo courtesy Berkeley County Historical Society

A brand new Martinsburg High School, which Ethel and her classmates entered as freshmen in 1928. The facility was heralded at the time as "one of the best equipped high schools in this section of the country."

Each member wore a red, white and blue corsage or boutonniere, a gift from class member Ethel Lewis Thurston and fashioned by her daughter Shirley Faye.

The class is proud of having entered the "new" high school as freshmen in the fall of 1928 and being the first class to attend there all four years. We graduated in the spring of 1932 with 142 members, the largest class up to that time.

The Great Depression was in full swing, and the class was not permitted by the Chamber of Commerce to seek advertising from local businesses to finance the school yearbook, so that was the first time in 20 years that the Triangle was not published. This was a disappointment, but the journalism class, under the leadership of Miss Frances Harness (who later became Mrs. Paul Hammann), got to work and put out a senior issue of *The Orange and Black,* with class photos and information. A number of local businesses made its publication possible.

These important documents are real treasures for those so fortunate as to possess them. The ads themselves are interesting reading. One for J. C. Penney Company features silk crepe frocks for graduation activities in "styles hard-to-please daughters will rave about," for $2.98 and $3.98.

To put this into perspective, we need to realize that in 1932 many people worked a full 10-hour day for $1.50 or less. My junior prom dress was a green flowered silk chiffon with a fish-tail hemline and cost $4.98 at the Union Store. I worked in the woolen mill the next summer, so for the Alumni Banquet my senior year I had a white eyelet-embroidered ankle-length dress with pink taffeta underskirt and a wide pink sash. It came from Emmert's and cost $10. I felt quite elegant.

Reunions were staged every five years from the 20th to the 50th, and have been annual events since that time. There are some 30 living members, but not all can attend the reunions. Leon Sperow, of Media, Pennsylvania, and his wife, Betty, who regularly attend, sent regrets. Leon had a serious heart attack and now has a pacemaker. They were in the process of moving to a more convenient home and hoped to be with us the following year. Anne Horsfall Auld was recuperating after having hip replacement surgery. We wish them the best.

All were saddened by the loss of Sarah Clendening Fry, who mailed in her reservation, then passed away unexpectedly a few days later. Our sympathy goes to her family.

Those who can make it come from

their own homes or from assisted living quarters, but all share the same enthusiasm and eagerness to be with longtime friends for an afternoon of reminiscing and catching up on the news of their classmates' latest interests and activities.

I'd like to share some of the thoughts expressed by the late *Journal* Editor Paul B. Martin, one of the members of our class, in an editorial written after our 50-year reunion in 1982:

> **Attending a class reunion is an experience which can be described only by a person who has participated in one, because it runs the gamut of emotions—gladness, sadness, wistfulness, retrospection, what might have been.**
>
> **I have always liked to brag about that class (of course, everyone thinks his own class is something special) because of the camaraderie and the sort of espirit de corps that has been maintained for half a century and because practically all of its members turned out to be good citizens.**
>
> **Most of us never made much money, although I could count at least four millionaires present last week. None of us ever went on to national or international greatness, but nearly all assumed useful roles in society, made a contribution and hopefully are leaving the world a little better place in which to live.**

He went on to give the number in the class as 142, including 77 girls and 65 boys, and stated all but 30 members were still living at the time of the 50th reunion.

> **The class came out of school at the depth of the Depression and thus jobs were hard to find and not too many had enough money to go to college. Less than 10 years later the nation was plunged into WWII and by my own estimated count, more than half of the 65 boys went into some sort of military service for their country, many of them ending the war as officers.**
>
> **Most of the surviving class members have spent their lives in the Eastern Panhandle or nearby Maryland or**

Photo from author's collection

Graduates of Martinsburg High School Class of 1932 attending their 70-year reunion in 2002. Seated, left to right, are Frances Edwards Keller, J. Robert Brumbaugh, Donald Hill, and Ethel Lewis Thurston. Standing, Gyrl Lou Miller McIntyre, Elsie Catrow, Bernadine Knadler Rick, Allene Rinker Sullivan, Fred B. Hess, Anna Psalidas Widmyer, Ethel Wayble Bovey, Ruth Darby Dean, Ruth Lee Thompson Bauserman, and Mildred Rockwell O'Rourke.

Virginia, so that it has been possible to remain in relatively close touch. They went into many fields of endeavor, including the ministry, engineering, education, farming, nursing, business and various trades such as newspaper work. At least three attained professional rank in colleges and two hold doctoral degrees.

Those who remained here branched out into many forms of community service, including leadership positions in fraternal, civic and professional organizations. No less than eight members of the class, for example, became president of the Martinsburg High School Alumni Association.

In the field of public service locally, one man became chief of the Martinsburg Fire Department, one served a number of years on the Berkeley County Board of Education, one was mayor of the city, three served on the City Council, one was the first woman to be elected a jus-

tice of the peace here, and another became the first woman to serve on the board of directors of a Martinsburg bank.

After several nostalgic recollections, Martin closed with:

Yes, I'm very proud to have been a member of that class of 1932 because it has been a true cross-section of all of the best that this great country represents.

Buck didn't mention that he was named Outstanding Alumnus by the Martinsburg High School Alumni Association, that he was the one who was elected mayor at age 31, and that he was the first of three members of the class who received Outstanding West Virginian citations. That editorial is a fine tribute to the Class of 1932, and a true picture of the relationship that still exists among those who make a special effort to get together for our annual reunion.

I gave the class response at the Alumni Banquet the following night at the high school, issuing a couple of challenges:

I'm happy to bring congratulations to the Class of 2002 and greetings to all of you from the Class of 1932. I know you graduates will receive a lot of advice tonight, so I'll keep mine brief. Whether you continue your schooling or not—never stop learning. Keep your faith in the Lord, and keep alert for opportunities to learn.

The Class of 1932 celebrated our 70-year reunion yesterday afternoon at Heritage Hall, and it was a blast. (After 70 years, you tend to do your celebrating in the afternoon.) We had 14 class members and 16 guests. Guests were family members, friends and caregivers. Remember, we're all in our upper 80s! I used to think that was really OLD!

Now, to you other folks I say, never stop living! I'm working hard to re-invent the image of aging. What is aging, but living a longer life? We're only as old as we let ourselves think we are. We can sit around and feel sorry for ourselves if we want to, but what's the fun in that?

Maybe we can't do everything we once did, but we can always do something! Just keep that in mind. So, do you

know what? I polish my partials and my tri-focals, put in my hearing aids, get my walker in gear—and head out to where the action is! I still have a lot of living to do! And so do you!

In closing, I sincerely hope you have enjoyed reading my *Hometown Memories* as much as I have enjoyed writing about the people, places, and events and sharing my personal experiences growing up in Martinsburg, West Virginia.

—Ethel Wayble Bovey

Honored West Virginian

In October 2003, Ethel Wayble Bovey was named Honored West Virginian of 24th Annual Mountain State Apple Harvest Festival and rode through the streets of her hometown in the Grand Feature Parade. This honor marks a lifetime of accomplishments, but her story does not end here. Now 88-years-old, the writer defies physical conditions that make mobility difficult and remains an inspiration to others, from giving motivational talks to planning an Alaskan cruise with her friends.

Photo from author's collection

Ethel Wayble Bovey with daughter Sharilyn.